THE BAR/BAT MITZVAH PLANBOOK

Also by Ellen Epstein and Jane Lewit

*Record and Remember: Tracing Your
Roots Through Oral History*

THE BAR/BAT MITZVAH PLANBOOK

Revised Edition

Jane Lewit and Ellen Epstein

SCARBOROUGH HOUSE

SCARBOROUGH HOUSE

Published in the United States of America
by Scarborough House
4720 Boston Way
Lanham, Maryland 20706

Distributed by NATIONAL BOOK NETWORK

Tikkun page reprinted with the permission of KTAV Publishing House,
Inc., from *Tikkun Lahkori'im* (Revised Edition), copyright © 1946 by
Fannie Scharfstein, copyright © 1969 by KTAV Publishing House, Inc.

The *Bar/Bat Mitzvah Planbook* was originally published in hardcover
by Stein and Day/*Publishers*, and has been updated for this edition.

Illustrations by Yowa

Library of Congress Cataloging-in-Publication Data

Lewit, Jane.
The Bar/Bat Mitzvah planbook / Jane Lewit and Ellen Epstein
foreword by Joshua O. Haberman.—Rev. ed.
p. cm.
Includes index.
1. Bar mitzvah. 2. Bat mitzvah. I. Epstein, Ellen Robinson.
II. Title.
BM707.L48 1996 296.4'424—dc20 93-34017 CIP

ISBN 0-8128-8546-5 (pbk: alk. paper)

Printed in the United States of America

⊖™ The paper used in this publication meets the minimum requirements of
American National Standard for Information Sciences—Permanence of
Paper for Printed Library Materials, ANSI Z39.48–1984.

Contents

Why hold the ceremony at all/ The tradition of the Bar Mitzvah at age thirteen/ The Bat Mitzvah

At what age does a child become Bar/Bat Mitzvah?/ Your child's Hebrew birthdate/ The yearly cycle of readings: the Torah and Haftarah portions/ The Jewish holiday calendar/ Jewish holidays with their special festivities/ Jewish days of remembrance with certain limitations/ Secular holidays, vacation times, the weather, and other factors

Vocabulary of the Bar/Bat Mitzvah service/ The Shabbat morning service and kiddush/ The Friday evening service and Oneg Shabbat/ Mincha and Havdalah/ Other services: A Monday or Thursday Torah service, Rosh Hodesh, a festival

PREPARING YOUR CHILD

Basic training/ Individualized tutoring/ Study aids/ D'rash, Bar/Bat Mitzvah speech, personal prayer/ Understanding the synagogue service/ Tips for success/ The importance of a Jewish education/ Education for the child with special needs/ Creative Bar/ Bat Mitzvah courses of study/ The Jewish home transmitting Jewish values/ Suggestions for those starting late

SHARING THE HONORS

Aliyah—being called to the Torah/ Grandparents and their participation/ Special family situations/ Hagbah and Glilah/ Sharing the spotlight with siblings

PROVIDING THE TRADITIONAL RITUAL ITEMS

Head coverings/ Tallit: A prayer shawl with Tzitzit (fringes)/ Selecting a tallit/ Tefillin/ Other ritual items: candlesticks, kiddush cup, challah cover

THE INVITATION

Standard printed invitations/ Designing your own invitation/ Parents who are separated or divorced/ Additional inserts and the RSVP/ Mailing the invitations

GUESTS

THE GUEST LIST: Whom to invite/ Completing the guest list

OUT-OF-TOWNERS: Lodging: Home hospitality or hotel reservations/ Providing for guests who observe kashrut/ Friday night dinner/ Sunday brunch/ Maps, directions and schedules for the weekend/

Explaining the service/ Providing baby-sitting/ Providing for guests who are Shomer Shabbat/ Some considerations for Orthodox and/or Conservative congregations

The party celebrating a Bar/Bat Mitzvah/ Suggestions for enhancing your party/ The type of celebration: Number of guests, children, and other variables/ Facilities where the reception may be held: synagogue, home, hotel, or club/ Serving the food: A buffet versus a served meal, or how are you going to feed all those invited guests?/ Planning the menu/ The synagogue and its kitchen: Kashrut and a mashgiach/ Basic checklist/ Flowers and centerpieces/ Music and singing/ Photography/ Cost-cutting hints/ Ideas for providing for your youngest guests

Gifts with Jewish meaning/ Unusual Jewish gifts/ A trip to Israel/ Tzedakah/ Remembering your synagogue/ The thank you note: Taking the time to respond properly and promptly

Holding the ceremony in Israel: The Kotel (Western Wall), atop Masada, or elsewhere/ Bat Torah/ Nontraditional settings/ The adult Bar/Bat Mitzvah

Bar/Bat Mitzvah Timetable: Countdown to a Simcha/ Preliminary Family List/ Preliminary List of Friends of the parents/ Preliminary List of Your Child's Friends/ Preliminary List of Members of Your Congregation/ Preliminary List of Professional and

Business Associates/   Preliminary List of Neighbors/
Final Guest List/   Aliyot and Honors Chart

Acknowledgments

As our book goes to print, we recognize how many people helped us to develop the original version and to completely update our fourth paperback edition. Friends, parents, Jewish professionals, bar/bat mitzvah students themselves from Adelaide, Australia to San Jose, California helped us with interesting questions, personal concerns, and creative suggestions. We are deeply grateful to each of them. We especially appreciate the efforts of many rabbis, cantors, and educators who reviewed the manuscript to assure that our information is relevant for today's bar/bat mitzvah families.

We thank our children Abigail, Benjamin, and Phoebe Lewit, along with Jeremy, Asher, Barak, and Dina Epstein who allowed us to test our principles in practice as they turned thirteen. One more opportunity awaits us at Kira Epstein's upcoming Bat Mitzvah. An extra word of thanks to Abby Lewit, whose Bat Mitzvah inspired this book and to Jessica Levine, whose editorial help has been invaluable, and to special needs experts, Sara Rubinow Simon and Sara Portman Milner. And, of course, we can never overlook our husbands, Robert Lewit and David Epstein, who supported our project, laughed with us and understood our unique work schedule.

Foreword

It gives me great pleasure to write the foreword to the completely revised fourth edition of *The Bar/Bat Mitzvah Planbook*. Rarely does a book come along which so well fits the needs of our contemporary Jewish families. In step-by-step fashion, the book clearly explains the history, traditions, and vocabulary of the bar/bat mitzvah. In addition, it answers your questions about how to prepare for your child's ceremony and celebration.

Jane Lewit and Ellen Epstein, two experienced and professional authors, mothers, and bar/bat mitzvah planners, give you a blueprint for an easy, stress-free bar or bat mitzvah. They have thought of everything from *Havdalah* to handicap access, from computer tutors to *challah* covers. Their quick and handy guide offers specific ideas to use immediately and creative suggestions to help you personalize your celebration. Most important, Jane and Ellen share the hope that each bar/bat mitzvah will joyfully celebrate this rite of passage and feel more deeply connected to his or her family, community, and Jewish heritage.

Rabbi Joshua O. Haberman
President, Foundation for Jewish Studies
Washington, D.C.

Preface

Mazel tov ! You are embarking on a wonderful life cycle event.

As every Jewish child comes of age, the entire Jewish People celebrates. The Bar/Bat Mitzvah represents the renewal of the community because each child links the majestic Jewish past with the potential for a dynamic and meaningful future.

As parents and as teachers we strive to build memories that will last a lifetime. We seek those "teachable moments" when parents and educators have an influence and the child is receptive. The rituals of Bar/Bat Mitzvah provide times of joy and achievement, laughter and learning that can stimulate a deep attachment to the Jewish people.

Jane Lewit and Ellen Epstein—colleagues and friends—provide their readers with invaluable information about the many aspects of preparing for a Bar/Bat Mitzvah. They are sensitive to the varying knowledge levels and religious perspectives of those using their guidebook. What is most important to me is their emphasis on the significance of the occasion when a young person can feel the love of family and the warmth of tradition.

By using this planbook you will find helpful advice and creative suggestions for passing Jewish traditions from generation to generation!

Dr. Shulamith Reich Elster
Associate Professor of Jewish Education
Baltimore Hebrew University
Baltimore, MD

Introduction

Help! Help! My Child is Having a Bar/Bat Mitzvah.

How-to books answer questions of every sort from how to gain more storage space in your closet to how to prepare for the SAT examinations. But when a young Jewish parent is faced by the one or two year countdown to a bar/bat mitzvah, what easy-to-read guide can they consult? *The Bar/Bat Mitzvah Planbook* answers questions for parents from whatever their Jewish background. It is written by parents for parents. It is based on our personal experience planning for seven of our children (and one to go), consultations in our community, and feedback from parents around the country. The book is filled with practical advice, necessary information, cost-cutting hints, background data, and a complete glossary of bar/bat mitzvah terms. All words appearing in *italics* in the text can be found in the Glossary at the back of the book.

Underlying the planning is the assumption that the bar/bat mitzvah ceremony and celebration mark a passage in the life of the child where values are being transmitted from generation to generation. How can this best be done? We have specific suggestions for:

- preparing your child
- choosing a date
- understanding the service
- selecting or designing the invitation
- acquiring the appropriate ritual items
- organizing your guest list (with charts and timetables)
- providing hospitality for your guests
- extending the festivities with a party
- alternatives for the ceremony and celebration

Children are preparing for this ceremony from many different backgrounds, reflecting the breadth of the American Jewish community today. We realize that some readers will know a little more, some a little less. Therefore, some of you will find it useful to read every page of this guide; others may dip into it here and there to help clarify one point or another. Wherever your family finds itself along this spectrum, you can be comfortable knowing that there are many others like you, who are offering this special opportunity to their children. The rich heritage of Judaism encompasses a variety of religious beliefs and traditions. While some customs are commonly followed, there is a great diversity in practice. This planbook should serve as a helpful guide in organizing your Bar/Bat Mitzvah. It is not intended to give a single answer but, rather, to suggest what can be done. You have the opportunity to choose what is relevant and meaningful. We suggest that you consult your rabbi, religious school director, or other leaders in your congregation to guide your decisions. With this planbook in hand, you can now anticipate your child's Bar/Bat Mitzvah with joy. Here's how to do it.

Bar/Bat Mitzvah Background

Bar/Bat Mitzvah Background

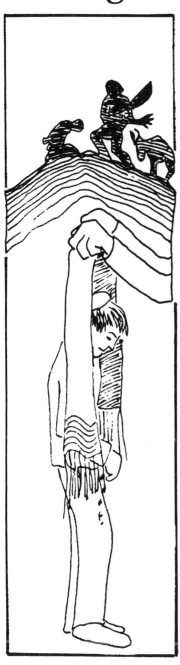

Why Hold the Ceremony at All?

Why should your child celebrate becoming a bar/bat mitzvah? Preparing for this ceremony, your child gains a sense of identity, personal achievement, and self-confidence. Judaism is more than a religion; it is a way of living which enhances life. By learning its literature, language, prayers, and customs, a youngster can share more fully in his heritage. Studying for the bar/bat mitzvah ceremony gives your child a chance to learn and to grow and to take pride in these accomplishments. On his or her big day, friends and family acknowledge what he has done, which can include anything from designing the invitation to "twinning" his ceremony with an Ethiopian Jew in Israel.

Equally important is the use of ritual to celebrate the transition from one stage of life to another. We recognize, as did our ancestors, the importance of punctuating our life cycle with ceremony. The bar/bat mitzvah is a very moving experience, often having a profound effect on the young person.

If you are ambivalent, skeptical or even against holding the ceremony, we encourage you to give it another thought. Some parents recall their own trying or boring religious school training and do not want to impose a similar experience on their children. Remember, this is a new generation with high-tech teaching methods and plenty of lively materials for the classroom. Or you may feel social pressure to hold an event which does not appeal to you, such as the family who took over Yankee Stadium. Clearly, your celebration can be creatively personalized without getting out of control. Some parents have told us that they regretted not giving their children a Jewish education and bar/bat mitzvah preparation. So, encourage your son or daughter to experience his Jewish heritage through the bar/bat mitzvah.

In fact, your child's coming of age is not a private

3

moment, but one of significance for the entire Jewish community. Passing on Jewish tradition is essential if our rich heritage is to be perpetuated. A *midrash* tells of a despot who asked, "How can we overcome the Jewish people?" The perceptive reply of his councilor was, "Go up and down before their houses of study and houses of worship. If you do not hear the voices of children chanting, you can overcome them. But, if you hear the chant of children, you will never subdue them."[1] It is said that the pillars on which the world stands are its children. All this reflects how the hopes of the parents and the expectations of the community rest on the promise of the next generation.

The child enters a new stage in life, as he identifies with the adult Jewish community and commits himself to lead a responsible Jewish life. The Jewish community rejoices because it is renewed and strengthened by the bar/bat mitzvah. All groups within the American Jewish community, Orthodox, Conservative, Reform, and Reconstructionist, view the bar/bat mitzvah as important. Today, parents from varied backgrounds, with different levels of Jewish knowledge and identity, are preparing their children.

---

1. Azriel Eisenberg, ed., *Bar Mitzvah Treasury* (New York: Behrman House, 1969), p. 301.

The Tradition of the Bar Mitzvah at Age Thirteen

Why does a child become a bar/bat Mitzvah at age thirteen? The origins of this ceremony are obscure and are not mentioned specifically in the Torah. The *Talmud* records that at the time of the Second Temple (520 B.C.E.– 70 C.E.), it was traditional for the sages to bless a child who had reached the age of thirteen and who had fasted on Yom Kippur. A *midrash* tells us that Abraham was thirteen when he heeded God's call to leave his father's home, turn from idol worship, and enter into a personal covenant with God. Similarly, the twins, Jacob and Esau, reached the critical turning point in their lives at age thirteen. It was then that they separated—Jacob to study the Torah and become known as Israel, and Esau to follow the ways of idolatry. In Genesis 34:25 "Simeon and Levi . . . took each *man* his sword . . ." According to Rabbinic tradition, Levi was thirteen when he was referred to as a man, thus marking the transition between boyhood and adulthood.

The *Pirke Avot* describes fundamental Jewish teachings in epigrammatic form. It says:

> At five years, the age is reached for the study of Scripture; at ten, for the study of *Mishnah*; at thirteen, for the fulfillment of the commandments . . .   [5:24]

By the time the *Talmud* was compiled in the sixth century of the Common Era rabbis universally recognized that the thirteen-year-old was obligated to follow the commandments and be responsible for his actions. At that time, a thirteen-year-old male was also viewed as an adult, in terms of legal matters. His vow was valid and he could participate in a *Bet Din*. Giving further authority to this ceremony, the sage Rashi stated that Bar Mitzvah should be considered as obligatory as the biblical laws given at Sinai.

Perhaps the significance of age thirteen was influenced by earlier puberty rites. By the second century Eleazar ben Simon noted that a father was responsible for his son only up to age thirteen. Thirteen typically marked the onset of sexual maturity, a time when childhood was left behind. The sages of the *Mishnah* added a spiritual dimension to this purely physical change. They noted that the threshold of thirteen for a boy, and twelve for a girl, brought with it not only puberty but also the *yetzer hatov*, or good inclination. No longer would a child's behavior solely be dominated by instinct and inclination for evil, *yetzer hara*. He is now guided by his own spiritual strength and therefore responsible for his behavior and the consequences of his actions. Therefore, a parent can recite a benediction at his child's bar/bat Mitzvah, *Baruch shepetarani me'onsho shel zeh*, or Blessed is He who has freed me from responsibility for this child's conduct. Now the child's moral sense is deemed to be sufficiently developed for him to know right from wrong.

In the late Middle Ages, the Bar Mitzvah evolved into a form which closely resembles the ceremony of today. It developed within the context of Judaism as a community-based religion. The Bar Mitzvah was a public demonstration of a youngster's new role as a member of the adult Jewish community with the obligations and privileges that this entailed. The celebration was marked when the Torah was read the first time after the child's thirteenth birthday. Thus, the tradition of Bar Mitzvah at thirteen was firmly rooted.

In Eastern Europe, the ceremony usually took place as the boy was called up to the Torah on a Monday or Thursday. A significant part of the ritual was putting on *tefillin* for prayer. In Western Europe, the Bar Mitzvah was usually on Shabbat, with the boy being called up to the Torah to read the *Maftir*, the final portion, and the accompanying *Haftarah* from the Prophets. In Germany, customs developed further, with boys conducting part or all of the synagogue service and possibly reading the full Torah portion of the week. Interestingly, for the *Marranos* of Spain and Portugal, who had to live as secret Jews, Judaism was first introduced to the next generation at Bar Mitzvah age, since it was felt that a boy of thirteen could be trusted to be discreet. In this way, with only secret observance, a Jewish heritage was preserved for over 300 years. In the dark years of World War II, Jewish families in Nazi-controlled Europe did not have the opportunity to mark life's passages. One and one-half million Jewish children were killed in the Nazi death factories. The promise of their youth was never realized.

Today, Jewish families are free to structure the bar/bat mitzvah as they choose. Literally, the term bar/bat mitzvah means son/daughter of the commandments and, according to Jewish tradition, one does not have to do anything to mark the occasion. A Jewish child automatically achieves the status of bar or bat mitzvah upon turning thirteen. From that age onward (in Orthodox synagogues, age twelve for girls), a Jewish person is counted as a responsible member of the community. However, many children and their parents choose to have a communal ceremony and celebration, sharing their joy with family and friends.

The Bat Mitzvah

The ceremony of Bat Mitzvah is a relatively recent addition to Jewish practices. (The word is pronounced "baht" in *Sephardic* Hebrew and "bahs" in *Ashkenazic* Hebrew.) Jewish tradition acknowledged that girls reached religious maturity at age twelve, although there was no specific ritual to mark their coming of age. However, in New York City on Saturday morning, May 6, 1922, a historic event took place at the Society for the Advancement of Judaism. Here at the center for the Reconstructionist movement, then a branch of Conservative Judaism, the eldest daughter of Rabbi Mordecai Kaplan became the first American girl to experience a Bat Mitzvah ceremony. It was an experimental moment in evolving ritual, with Rabbi Kaplan chanting the *maftir* and *haftarah* and Judith reciting the first blessing and reading the Torah selection from her own *chumash*.

Previously, under Rabbi Kaplan's leadership, his followers had begun to count women as part of the *minyan* needed for a prayer service. The growth of women's rights in this period had led to the passage of the Nineteenth Amendment to the United States Constitution in 1920 which granted women the right to vote. In America, the time was ripe for the Bat Mitzvah to take its place alongside the longer established Bar Mitzvah. Offering the Bat Mitzvah ceremony was an effort to give a Jewish girl an opportunity comparable to that of a Jewish boy. Over the years, the Bat Mitzvah has become an accepted tradition in many synagogues. Today many congregations offer one course of instruction for all children, culminating in either a Bar or a Bat Mitzvah ceremony. The service is the same, with the young person called to chant from the Torah and *Haftarah*.

However, other congregations feel that different rules should apply for girls and boys. Egalitarianism does not necessarily mean that Jewish women and men have identical religious roles. Distinctions are meant to be understood in a positive way for they reflect the congregation's interpretation of the separate functions for women and men within the Jewish community. Following this belief, some synagogues hold the Bat Mitzvah ceremony only on Friday night. Sometimes girls are allowed more latitude to develop a creative Bat Mitzvah observance, perhaps not possible in the prescribed nature of the usual Bar Mitzvah ceremony. Chanting the *Book of Esther* on *Purim* or leading a *Tu b'Shevat* service with its special prayers and songs are two innovative alternatives. Others encourage young women to demonstrate their achievement and commitment by delivering a learned speech or Torah discussion, known as a *d'rash* or *d'var Torah*. These celebrations often do not take place in the synagogue. Occasionally, such a ceremony is known as a "Bat Torah," marking a girl's coming of age though not identifying the rite of passage with the Bar Mitzvah.

Clearly, Judaism has changed in many different ways to accommodate the concept of Bat Mitzvah. Many older Jewish women are seeking to experience the Bat Mitzvah ceremony, which was not available to them in their youth. Hence, there is a growing movement for adult Bat Mitzvah classes throughout American Judaism today. Much has happened since the early 1920's when Rabbi Mordecai Kaplan referred to his four daughters as "four good reasons" to institute the Bat Mitzvah as part of Jewish ritual.

NOTES:

Choosing the Date

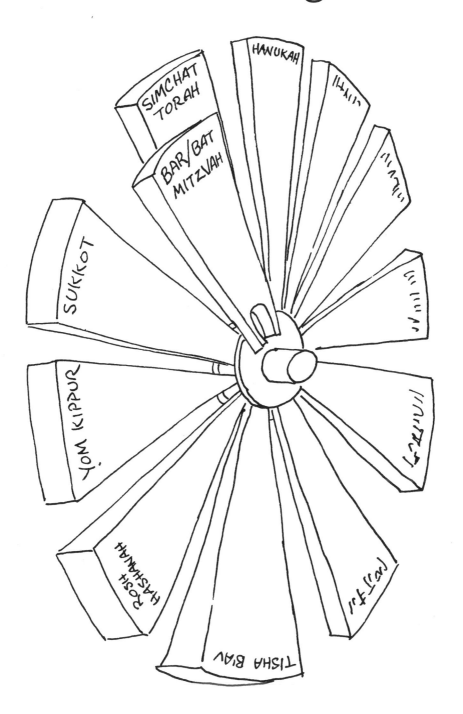

Choosing the Date

Many congregations give parents the opportunity to request a Bar/Bat Mitzvah date or to list several possible choices. Some congregations have so many children reaching the age of Bar/Bat Mitzvah at the same time that they cannot schedule the ceremony on the Shabbat following each child's birthday. While a Friday night or Saturday morning Bar/Bat Mitzvah is most common, it is also possible to hold this ceremony at a different service. Your synagogue leaders may be willing to consider options for a Bar/Bat Mitzvah to be held on Shabbat afternoon, a festival morning, or other times that services are customarily held in your synagogue. It typically is the role of congregational leaders or someone designated for that job to decide when each Bar/Bat Mitzvah is to be scheduled. A friend of ours who sets the Bar/Bat Mitzvah schedule for his synagogue acknowledges that coordinating the various requests requires the patience of Job and the wisdom of Solomon. If you are able to request a Bar/Bat Mitzvah date rather than having one assigned, here are some factors to consider.

At What Age Does a Child Become Bar/Bat Mitzvah?

It is customary for a boy to celebrate his Bar Mitzvah at age thirteen. In Jewish tradition, this age was viewed as the beginning of religious responsibility. Girls, who usually mature earlier, were considered to reach this point at age twelve. Some congregations today insist that all children experience this ceremony at the same age—thirteen. This also serves to keep a balanced religious school program with all students moving to the level of Bar/Bat Mitzvah when they are in the same school grade. You should check with your own synagogue leaders to find out how they view the Bat Mitzvah date. Do they schedule the ceremony as early as the twelfth birthday, the thirteenth birthday, or some date in between? If you have some flexibility here, consider the maturity of your own daughter and her readiness for the Bat Mitzvah experience, which marks her coming of age.

Whether for a daughter or a son, many parents have independently noted that significant growth takes place after a child has experienced the Bar/Bat Mitzvah process: the study, the preparation, and the synagogue ceremony. In addition to the physical changes which may be taking place at this time, the religious passage is accompanied by an emotional and psychological maturation on the part of the young teenager. This confirms the great wisdom and insight in Jewish tradition which marks this age for a public religious ceremony. The timing acknowledges the many changes which occur in this transitional period. The experience thus has a profound impact on the Bar/Bat Mitzvah as he or she enters adolescence.

Your Child's Hebrew Birthdate

In the Jewish calendar, months are calculated according to the cycle of the moon, but the year is determined according to the sun. This differs significantly from the Gregorian calendar used in the Western world. To learn your child's Hebrew birthdate, consult a perpetual Hebrew-English calendar which can be found at your synagogue or a Jewish book store. In addition, the index volume of the *Encyclopedia Judaica* or various Judaic software programs will have this information.

You will need to check the year of your child's birth. Look for the month and day on the secular calendar and see the corresponding Jewish month and date. Remember that Jewish days are counted from sundown to sundown so that if your child was born after dark, use the following day on the Jewish calendar. Working with your Hebrew date, find its thirteenth anniversary on the Hebrew calendar and its corresponding secular date. Now you will know when your child turns thirteen according to Jewish tradition.

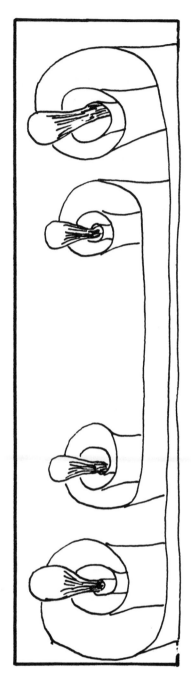

The Yearly Cycle of Readings: The Torah and Haftarah Portions

The Torah is divided into portions so that a different section is read each week; the entire cycle of readings fills a calendar year. At the holiday *Simchat Torah,* on the 23rd of Tishri, Jews celebrate completing the reading of the Torah scroll while beginning the next cycle without interruption. Each week, along with the specified Torah portion, there is a selection known as the Haftarah, from the Prophets, or *Nevi'im.*

In many congregations, the Bar/Bat Mitzvah child chants the *Maftir,* the final section from the week's Torah portion, and the accompanying *Haftarah.* This pattern of participation is traditional, having evolved in this form approximately 500 years ago. Publicly reading from the Torah and *Haftarah* is a demonstration of preparation and commitment to the Jewish community.

A Hebrew-Civil calendar can tell you which Torah portion is scheduled for each week of the year. A *Chumash* typically will have an index listing the names of all the Torah portions in order. In looking for a Chumash, it may be helpful to know the variety of words used to refer to this book. Chumash is a Hebrew word and comes from the same root as the Hebrew word for "five," *chamesh,* referring to the five Books of Moses. This is how the Torah also became known as the Pentateuch, from the Greek root for five. Below is a list of Torah portions in the annual cycle, starting from the beginning, Genesis. The names are derived from the first Hebrew word or words of each portion. After the name of each portion is a brief description of its contents.[1]

1. The descriptions were compiled from the following sources: "Adas Israel Chronicle," Adas Israel Congregation (Washington, D.C., 1979–1981). Arthur Chiel, *Guide to Sidrot and Haftarot,* Ktav (New York, 1971).

Description of Torah Portions

BOOK OF GENESIS/*BERESHIT*

1. BERESHIT Gen. 1–6:8

   This *sidra* begins with three simple but very important Hebrew words, *"Bereshit barah Elohim . . ."* "In the beginning God created . . ." Here is the most important teaching of Judaism: that there is a God and that He is the Creator of all life.

2. NOACH Gen. 6:9–11:32

   Unike other accounts of massive floods in primeval times, the biblical account alone underscores the ethical foundations of civilization. The world was destroyed because of selfishness.

3. LECH LECHA Gen. 12–17:27

   Abraham hears the call to leave his father's house, to search for a new way of life.

4. VAYYERA Gen. 18–22

   Abraham's love of God is tested. He is impelled to offer his son as a sacrifice, which God rejects. The rejection of human sacrifice is a milestone in the growth of civilization.

5. CHAYYE SARAH Gen. 23–25:18

   This *sidra* describes the life of Abraham and Sarah, his wife, including his purchase of a burial plot in Hebron. It also mentions Rebecca at the well.

6. TOLEDOT Gen. 25:19–28:9

   Esau sells his birthright for a bowl of soup and thereby creates a metaphor for repudiating one's potentialities. Jacob acquires his father's blessing.

7. VAYYETZE Gen 28:10–32:3

   Jacob lies down, tired, under the open sky, to sleep. He dreams a remarkable dream. It was a dream that gave Jacob the faith that God is everywhere and cares for the well-being of man. It gave him new hope for his life ahead.

8. VAYYISHLACH Gen. 32:4–36

   Jacob wrestled with God's messenger. He is thereupon renamed Israel, "He who has striven with God and with men, and has prevailed."

9. VAYYESHEV Gen. 37–40

   Joseph is sold into slavery by his jealous brothers. Despite every adversity, he never deviates from his faith in God.

10. MIKKETZ Gen. 41–44:17

    This *sidra* is a continuation of Joseph's experiences in Egypt. When Joseph's brothers appear before him, Joseph needs time to decide whether to make peace with them or to take vengeance for the past. He plans to test his brothers to see how they feel about their wrongdoing of long ago.

11. VAYYIGGASH Gen. 44:18–47:27

    Joseph, by now Prime Minister of Egypt, reveals his true identity to his brothers. Jacob and his sons take up residence in the land of Goshen.

12. VAYYECHI Gen. 47:28–50:26

    Jacob blesses his grandsons with words that Jewish parents say to their sons today, "May God make you as Ephraim and as Manasseh."

BOOK OF EXODUS/*SHEMOT*

1. SHEMOT Ex. 1–6:1
    In this sidra Moses has a vision while tending his flock one day near Mount Horeb. A voice speaks to him out of a burning bush. Moses is given a mission: He must return to Egypt to liberate the Israelite slaves with the assistance of God.

2. VA-AYRA Ex. 6:2–9
    God begins to bring plagues upon the land of Egypt, but Pharoah's heart will not be moved.

3. BO Ex. 10–13:16
    Upon suffering the tenth and most destructive plague, the smiting of the first born, Pharoah tells Moses and Aaron to take their people forth from Egypt.

4. BESHALLACH Ex. 13:17–17
    The Egyptian oppressors drown but "The children of Israel walked upon the dry land in the midst of the sea" reflecting the mighty hand of the Lord. This was the turning point separating the period of slavery from that of freedom.

5. YITHRO Ex. 18–20
    The Ten Commandments are revealed at Mt. Sinai amidst thunder and lightning. The Israelites tremble before God's power and majesty.

6. MISHPATIM Ex. 21–24
    This portion deals with many specific laws. We may deduce from this that it is inadequate to be a Jew "in general"; Judaism is lived in and through specific application.

7. TERUMAH Ex. 25–27:19
    The opening words of the sidra set the stage for our voluntary support of the Jewish community, "The Lord spoke to Moses, saying: 'Tell the Israelite people to bring Me offerings; you shall accept offerings for Me from every person whose heart so moves him.'"

8. TEZAVEH Ex. 27:20–30:10
    The *Ner Tamid,* or perpetual lamp, burning before the Ark, is described here. The rabbis interpret the lamp as a symbol of Israel, whose mission it was to become "a light of the nations." (Isaiah 42:6)

9. KI THISSA Ex. 30:11–34
    The Israelites forsake their God by worshipping a golden calf. Moses shatters the tablets of the Law when he beholds the people's idolatrous worship.

10. VAYYAKHEL Ex. 35–38:20
    The Israelites begin construction of the Tabernacle. Despite its sanctity, Moses admonishes the people that observance of the Sabbath takes precedence over the building of the Tabernacle, "On six days work may be done, but on the seventh day you shall have a Sabbath of complete rest, holy to the Lord."

11. PEKUDEY Ex. 38:21–40
    This *sidra* describes the final steps in building Israel's first house of worship. This takes place in the wilderness at Sinai while the people are on their long march to the Promised Land. The tabernacle is to be portable so that it can be set up and taken down as the people move from one camping site to another.

BOOK OF LEVITICUS/*VAYYIKRA*

1. VAYYIKRA Lev. 1–5
   This portion details the law concerning sacrifices offered in the Sanctuary. After the times of the First and Second Temple, prayer replaced sacrifices as the form of worship.

2. TZAV Lev. 6–8
   This *sidra* tells the laws for sacrifices brought to the altar of the Sanctuary which was Israel's house of worship during their years of wandering in the wilderness. The idea was that God blesses man with crops and flocks and, in turn, man gives these gifts to God. This portion also describes the event in the sanctuary when Aaron, the first High Priest, and his sons were initiated into their holy assignment as priests, *Kohanim*.

3. SHEMINI Lev. 9–11
   This *sidra* contains laws concerning the purity and holiness of the people of Israel. The sacrifices which they are to bring to the sanctuary are only part of their obligation. They must also, as part of their religious observance, act in every way with a sense of holiness. Here are the beginnings of the religious laws dealing with kosher and nonkosher, as they pertain to eating as well as other areas of human activity.

4. THAZRIA Lev. 12–13
   This Torah portion deals with sickness and health, with what was considered clean and unclean. The physical well-being of the community was a sacred concern among the Israelites. Physical cleanliness and health were considered important in order to achieve spiritual well-being. From early in Jewish history, the care and treatment of the sick was considered of greatest importance for the community.

5. METZORA Lev. 14–15
   The *Kohanim* were given the responsibility for healing the sick, including leprosy and other skin ailments. How does this treatment of illness belong to religion? How we live, what we eat, what we think, how we act in our everyday life, according to Judaism, all of these are included in the religious life.

6. ACHAREY MOT Lev. 16–18
   Only on *Yom Kippur* could the High Priest enter the Holy of Holies which contained the Ark of the Covenant which in turn contained the Tablets of the Law. Neither the High Priest's plea for forgiveness nor other ritual acts could achieve final forgiveness for Israel. Each Israelite was required to fast and atone on this day. Together, the High Priest and Israel, in sincerity, sought to achieve forgiveness for sins.

7. KEDOSHIM Lev. 19–20
   This surveys the foundations of Judaism, summarizing some of the most important ethical teachings of the Torah. This *sidra* clearly states that Israel must consider life as sacred, "You shall be holy; for I, the Lord, your God, am holy." These ethical teachings are summarized in the proclamation, "You shall love him [the stranger] as yourself, for you were strangers in the land of Egypt."

8. EMOR Lev. 21–24
   This *sidra* includes the lesson that the weekly Shabbat and the holidays which come at different seasons of the year are intended to teach Israel the holiness of time. On these days, there is opportunity to stop work and business, pause, and consider life's meaning and purpose, and to be refreshed.

9. BEHAR Lev. 25–26:2

This *sidra* defines a remarkable approach to the relationship that should exist between man and the earth which gives him sustenance. Balance is to be achieved on the basis of faith that "the earth is the Lord's." Man is only given the privilege of using it to sustain him and therefore must never abuse the land.

10. BECHUKOTAI Lev. 26:3–27

Moses puts an important challenge before Israel—to choose the way of the Torah. Let Torah's laws be the basis for Israel's life and the people will live well and prosper, and there will be "peace in the land."

BOOK OF NUMBERS/*BAMIDBAR*

1. BAMIDBAR Num. 1–4:20

This reports in detail the taking of the census of all adult males of Israel in the second year after their exodus from Egypt. It also tells how the large number of men, women, and children were organized for encampment during their years of wandering. The Tabernacle was always placed in the center of the camp.

2. NASO Num. 4:21–7

Here is introduced the priestly benediction first spoken by Aaron and his sons in the Tabernacle of the wilderness of long ago. The *Birchat Kohanim* implores, "May the Lord bless you and keep you. May the Lord make his face to shine upon you and be gracious unto you. May the Lord lift his countenance to you and grant you peace."

3. BEHAALOTECHA Num. 8–12

Moses needed great faith and courage to carry out his task as Israel's leader in the face of recurring criticism and uprisings. That is the underlying message of this portion.

4. SHELACH Num. 13–15

Shelach tells the story of the spies sent to survey the land of Canaan in preparation for its conquest. They reported that it was good agricultural land, but so strongly fortified that the Israelites could not possibly conquer it. Lacking faith, they raised a protest against Moses. Bitterly disappointed, Moses, the great leader, pleaded to God to forgive the people. Moses' plea was accepted, but God decreed that this adult generation would never enter Canaan.

5. KORACH Num. 16–18

This *sidra* reports another uprising against Moses due to Korach's envy. Moses prayed to God that justice be done against the rebels, and they were punished with death. It was the only way that the Israelites could be made to understand that Moses was truly the leader of Israel and that Aaron was legitimately *Kohen ha-Gadol*.

6. CHUKKAT Num. 19–22:1

This portion tells of the death of Miriam and Aaron, Moses' sister and brother. This was a sad time in the life of Israel's great leader. It was a period when the wilderness generation was quickly passing, making way for the younger generation who were to be given the opportunity to enter the Promised Land.

7. BALAK Num. 22:2–25:9

This *sidra* tells of Israel's confrontation with the Moabites, a people through whose territory Israel wished to march peacefully on their way to Canaan. Seeking to fight Israel, Balak, the King of Moab, sought to have Israel cursed. Instead of being cursed, the Jews are given a blessing, including the famous words, "How goodly are your tents, oh Jacob, your dwelling places, oh Israel!"

8. PINCHAS Num. 25:10–30:1

Here, Moses is instructed to go up to Mt. Abarim, to get a good view of the Promised Land, since he was not permitted to cross over into it. Moses is also told to appoint Joshua as his successor to Israel's leadership. The appointment ceremony was to be public, so that when Moses died it would be clear in the people's mind that Joshua was their new leader.

9. MATTOT Num. 30:2–32

Having arrived east of the Jordan River, two tribes, Reuben and Gad, together with half of the tribe of Manasseh requested that they be permitted to settle there. Moses criticized them. Did they plan to separate themselves from the rest of Israel, who would be settling on the west side of the Jordan? The leaders of these tribes assured Moses that they were fully loyal and would share in every responsibility of Israel.

10. MASSEY Num. 33–36

This *sidra* reports on the wanderings of Israel from the time they left Egypt to the time they reached the borders of Canaan. It also gives a detailed description of what were to be the boundaries of the land of Israel.

BOOK OF DEUTERONOMY/*DEVARIM*

1. DEVARIM Deut. 1–3:22

This consists of Moses' farewell to Israel, delivered at the end of his long period as its leader. He was soon to die and wanted to use his remaining strength to review for Israel its history, its special relationship with God, and its future as a people.

2. VA-ETHCHANAN Deut. 3:23–7:11

Here, Moses continues his farewell to Israel, with a review of the Ten Commandments and an appeal not to forget what they experienced at Mt. Sinai. Moses then gives to Israel the great message of the *Shema*. Israel must hear as clearly as possible that there is but one God, have a deep love for Him, study His teachings carefully, and live by them inside and outside their homes. Moses warns Israel, as strongly as possible, that when they enter Canaan, they must live their own sacred way of life. They must not intermarry with any of the pagan people whom they will meet in Canaan. To do so would weaken Israel's covenant with God.

3. EKEV Deut. 7:12–11:25

What does God require of Israel for all His generosity to us? Nothing that is beyond the reach of each of us: only that we love and serve Him and live by the commandments which He revealed to us.

4. RE'EH Deut. 11:26–16:17

"Behold, I set before you this day a blessing and a curse: the blessing, if ye shall hearken unto the commandment of the Lord your God, which I command you this day; and the curse, if you shall not hearken . . ." The future depends on our making the right choice. To do right, we must follow the laws, which Moses now spells out in detail.

5. SHOFETIM Deut. 16:18–21:9

Justice must be carried out in the land which the Israelites will soon settle, "Justice,

justice must you follow, that you may live, and inherit the land which the Lord, your God, gives you."

6. KI THETZE Deut. 21:10–25

Moses reviews a variety of laws which are intended to strengthen family life and human decency in Israel. Parents are responsible for the education of their children. If one finds lost property, it must be returned to the owner. Accident prevention is obligatory for property owners. Kindness to animals is required by law. The community is responsible for the needs of strangers, widows, and orphans. The law requires honest business practices: weights and measures must be absolutely dependable.

7. KI THAVO Deut. 26–29:8

The people soon would be crossing the Jordan, and their first assignment was to write the code of laws by which they were to live, as a sign that this land was theirs in consequence of the covenant and on condition of carrying out the law. The second assignment, on entering the land, was to build an altar for public worship on which to bring peace offerings to God.

8. MITZAVIM Deut. 29:9–30

In Moses' third farewell address to Israel, he points out that all Israel is gathered for the completion of the covenant with God. It is binding upon all the generations of Israel that will follow for all time to come. The Torah and its teachings will be theirs as much as if they personally had received it at Sinai. The covenant is unending.

9. VAYYELECH Deut. 31

Here, Moses completes the writing of the Torah and entrusts it to the *Kohanim* and elders of Israel. He instructs them to read the Torah before the people at regular intervals. The Torah was not to remain the special preserve of the priests but was to be heard by and be familiar to all the people.

10. HAAZINU Deut. 32

At the beginning of his role as Israel's leader, Moses has sung a song of praise to God at the crossing of the Red Sea. Now, though he will soon die, Moses' faith in God is as strong as ever. He sings a final hymn of joy to God on the banks of the Jordan with the Promised Land on the horizon.

11. VEZOTH HA-BERACHAH Deut. 33–34

Before Moses goes up to the mountain top to have a brief look at Canaan, he blesses the tribes of Israel. He then goes up, dies, and is buried in the Valley of Moab. Israel mourns his passing deeply and turns to his successor, Joshua, for leadership.

If you may request a specific date and have reviewed the various Torah portions, here are some ideas to consider: Perhaps your child will want to read the same portion which his father or a favorite relative read at his Bar Mitzvah. Perhaps your youngster would like to read a section which includes his biblical namesake or other material of particular interest to him. But all the portions are valuable. One scholarly rabbi has said that every week he wants to say that this is the best, most important portion in the cycle. This reflects the fact that each section has its own significance, which becomes apparent when one has studied it with care.

The Jewish Holiday Calendar

The calendar below includes the major Jewish holidays. To learn which secular dates coincide with these Hebrew dates, or to know when other fast days and minor holidays occur, consult your rabbi or synagogue calendar.

FALL HOLIDAYS

Rosh Hashanah	1 Tishri	Jewish New Year
Yom Kippur	10 Tishri	Day of Atonement
Sukkot	15 Tishri	Harvest Festival; Feast of Tabernacles
Shemini Atzeret	22 Tishri	8th Day of Assembly
Simchat Torah	23 Tishri	Rejoicing with the Torah

WINTER HOLIDAYS

Chanukah	25 Kislev	Festival of Lights
Tu b'Shevat	15 Shevat	New Year of the Trees
Purim	14 Adar	Holiday of Lots

(In Hebrew years when there is an extra month of Adar II, Purim occurs on the 14th of Adar II.)

SPRING HOLIDAYS

Pesach	15 Nisan	Passover
Yom Ha-Shoah	27 Nisan	Holocaust Day
Yom Ha-Atzma'ut	3, 4, or 5 of Iyar	Israeli Independence Day
Lag b'Omer	18 Iyar	33rd Day in the Counting of the Omer.
Shavuot	6 Sivan	Feast of Weeks; Giving of the Ten Commandments

SUMMER HOLIDAYS

Tisha b'Av	9 Av	Destruction of the Temple

(When the 9th of Av falls on a shabbat, this fast day is moved forward to the 10th of Av.)

NOTE: There are many fine points to the Jewish calendar. Be sure to check with your rabbi before deciding on a date.

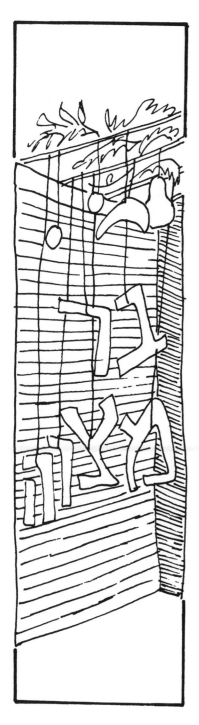

Jewish Holidays with Their Special Festivities

You may wish to check the Jewish holiday schedule during the season of your Bar/Bat Mitzvah by consulting a Hebrew calendar. Every holiday is marked by special religious rituals and is an occasion for joyous celebration. These observances and festivities would enhance any Bar/Bat Mitzvah ceremony. At *Sukkot, Chanukah,* the Shabbat before *Purim,* and certain other times during the year an extra Torah scroll is taken from the ark as part of the service. This may give you the opportunity to extend additional synagogue honors to your guests. Certain festivals, such as *Pesach* and *Sukkot,* may call for chanting the *Hallel,* prayers of praise which embellish the service. If it is a Jewish holiday, this may affect the readings at that service as well. To know the rituals observed at your synagogue, it is best to check with your rabbi, cantor, or other congregational leaders.

If your child's Bar/Bat Mitzvah falls at a holiday time, you will be able to enhance your celebration with the traditional rituals and foods appropriate to that occasion. At *Sukkot,* you could have your reception outdoors, either in your own or the synagogue's *sukkah,* decorated with the fruits, grains, and vegetables of that harvest festival. Several families we know had beautiful Bar Mitzvah receptions during Chanukah. They placed a *Chanukiah* as the centerpiece at each table, served potato latkes, and sang the songs customary for that season of rejoicing. In this and in many other ways, you can add an extra dimension of joy to your Bar/Bat Mitzvah celebration.

Jewish Days of Remembrance with Certain Limitations

There are certain days of remembrance in the Jewish calendar when you may not want to hold a Bar/Bat Mitzvah. It may be inappropriate to select times which commemorate tragic events in Jewish history. Among these is *Yom Ha-Shoah*, the day when we remember the lives of 6 million of our people who perished in the Holocaust. In the summer, at *Tisha b'Av*, we recall the destruction of the First and Second Temples. At this and at five other times in the Jewish calendar year, it has been traditional to fast. In addition, during the period from *Pesach* to *Shavuot*, during the counting of the *Omer*, there may be certain restrictions on having a Bar/Bat Mitzvah celebration. At *Pesach*, while basically a season of gladness, your reception could be affected by the prohibition against eating leavened foods. Consult with your rabbi as to how these special dates may affect you.

Secular Holidays, Vacation Times, the Weather, and Other Factors

Secular holidays, vacation times, and the weather may influence your request for a Bar/Bat Mitzvah date. Keep in mind that these factors will undoubtedly be secondary to other more important criteria.

Secular holidays can be a good time to schedule a Bar/Bat Mitzvah. This can affect your planning in several ways. When a secular holiday is observed on a Monday, this offers you a long weekend. If your child's Bar/Bat Mitzvah is on Shabbat, you then have an extra day for your guests to visit and/or travel home. If you belong to a synagogue where the Torah is read on Mondays and Thursdays, in addition to Saturday morning, this may give you the opportunity to schedule a complete Bar/Bat Mitzvah on a weekday.

You should keep in mind that secular and important Christian holidays may also affect your plans. For instance, if your child's Bar/Bat Mitzvah falls on New Year's weekend, you must consider if you will have a difficult time hiring help and scheduling a caterer. Determine if it will be difficult for your guests to plan travel arrangements and accommodations for that period. Ask yourself if there are other problems which may arise because of your Bar/Bat Mitzvah date.

Check whether your congregation schedules Bar/Bat Mitzvah ceremonies during July and August. In some congregations, summer services are held on a limited basis since many members as well as synagogue staff may be on vacation at that time. You may find that the Sisterhood is not available during these months to assist with your reception. Your child and/or his friends may go to overnight camp. Some of your guests may have planned summer trips far in advance. These may conflict with your Bar/Bat Mitzvah date. One family we know, in order to avoid this problem, sent post cards in December of the year preceding their child's August bat mitzvah. The post card alerted guests to "save the date." This technique also works well if your *simcha* will fall on Labor Day weekend. Sending a post card in June to family and friends will ensure that a greater number of guests will be available to come.

There may be other considerations. If you are likely to worry about the weather, you may not want to request February if you live in Boston or August if you live in Dallas. Elderly grandparents may prefer a date when the local climate is likely to be pleasant. If you can expect reasonable weather, your anxiety level will drop accordingly. Does your child have allergies every spring which cause his nose to run and his voice to go hoarse? Does your child have a good friend in another congregation who may be requesting the same Bar/Bat Mitzvah date? Is another close relative planning a wedding or 50th anniversary celebration within weeks of yours? Will this cause family members to choose between your *simcha* and someone else's? Are there any other circumstances which may influence your request in setting the Bar/Bat Mitzvah date?

When more than one child requests the same Bar/Bat Mitzvah date, two children may participate in a ceremony at the same service. In some large congregations, this is commonly done, because the calendar is crowded with children reaching age thirteen at the same time. We have been to services where two youngsters shared the occasion, each leading part of the service and reading sections from the *Haftarah* and Torah. This can be very satisfactory.

One family in Atlanta chose to have their twins share their ceremony with a newly discovered relative who had recently moved to New York from South Africa. The three young cousins were turning thirteen at the same time. They all gathered in Atlanta for a very special family occasion, the B'nai Mitzvot of their children and a large family reunion.

NOTES:

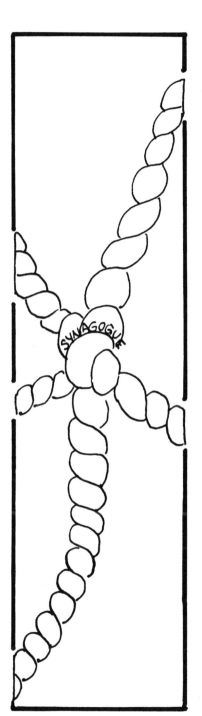

Understanding the
Synagogue Service

Understanding the Synagogue Service

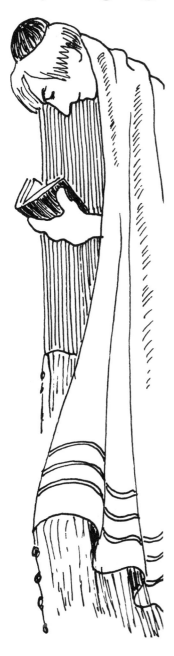

From the very start, Jewish worship was a communal experience. When the Temple in Jerusalem was destroyed and Jews were scattered throughout the world, the local synagogue became the place where the community gathers. In fact, the word *synagogue* is derived from two Greek words meaning "bring" and "together" or "assembly." While one may pray in private, there is special merit in praying with a congregation. Traditionally, one needs a *minyan*—a quorum of ten—to hold a worship service. Many of its commandments deal with interpersonal relationships. A person leads a Jewish life in relation to others; Judaism is not a religion of withdrawal or isolated spirituality. Supported by the congregation, one celebrates life's joys and bears its tragedies.

Holding the bar/bat mitzvah ceremony in the synagogue has been a long-standing tradition. Family and friends, the entire congregation rejoice as the child becomes a member of the community. In planning your child's bar/bat mitzvah, it is helpful to review some of the vocabulary of services within the synagogue.

Vocabulary of the Bar/Bat Mitzvah Service

ALIYAH: Being called up to the Torah to recite a blessing before and after the Torah is read.

AMIDAH: A central prayer said while standing.

ARON HA KODESH: Holy ark, where the Torah scrolls are kept in the synagogue.

BAR OR BAT MITZVAH: A rite of passage, generally at age thirteen, which signifies entry into the adult Jewish community.

BIMAH: The platform where the reader's stand for the Torah is placed. Often, the rabbi and cantor are on the bimah.

D'VAR TORAH: A learned speech on some aspect of the weekly Torah portion.

HAFTARAH: The reading from the Prophets following the Torah reading on the Sabbath and festivals.

HALLEL: Psalms of praise included in certain services.

KADDISH: In various forms, the most famous of which is the mourners' kaddish, it is used to separate sections of the service. The kaddish praises God, proclaims his sovereignty and affirms faith in God.

KIPPAH: A hat or head covering. Covering one's head follows an ancient Jewish tradition which signifies respect for God, specially in a house of worship.

MAFTIR: The concluding section of the weekly Torah portion, usually read by the bar/bat mitzvah child.

SHABBAT SHALOM: A customary greeting at the end of services, meaning "a peaceful sabbath."

SHEMA: The cardinal principle of Judaism, "Hear, O Israel, the Lord our God, the Lord is One."

SIDRA: The Torah portion of the week.

TALLIT: A prayer shawl, traditionally worn at services by men over thirteen. In some Reform and Conservative congregations, women may also wear a tallit.

TORAH: Narrowly defined, it is handwritten, parchment scroll containing the Five Books of Moses. It is the holiest object of the Jewish people. In the synagogue, it is kept in the ark and read during certain services.

The Shabbat Morning Service and Kiddush

It is common today and closely follows tradition for the Bar/Bat Mitzvah ceremony to occur at the Saturday morning synagogue service. This is what you probably visualize as the usual Bar/Bat Mitzvah experience. With roots back in the Middle Ages, this has been the setting where the child publicly affirms his commitment to fulfill the responsibilities of an adult member of his Jewish community. It is here that he is allowed to participate in the rituals associated with religious maturity. He is called up to the Torah for an *aliyah* for the first time. To demonstrate his interest and learning, it is customary for the child to read the *Maftir,* the concluding section from the Torah portion for the week, and the accompanying *Haftarah* from the prophetic literature. If the child is particularly able and interested, he may lead part or all of the service, or do more of the Torah reading for that week. Your synagogue may prescribe the extent to which a Bar/Bat Mitzvah may participate in leading the service. Check with your rabbi or ritual leaders for that information.

In some synagogues, blessings are said over the *challah* and wine directly after the service. The entire congregation is usually included at this kiddush. The kiddush could be anything from a simple meal with foods such as herring, gefilte fish, and cookies, or an elaborate spread including smoked salmon, pasta salads, kugels, and cakes. The purpose is to share fellowship with other members of the synagogue community.

The Friday Evening Service and Oneg Shabbat

Some congregations offer girls the choice of Friday evening or Saturday morning for their bat mitzvah service. Other congregations may insist on Friday evening where the young woman may say the blessings over the candles, chant *kiddush,* say prayers, and assist in leading the service. Usually there is no Torah service on Friday evening. However, we do know a few synagogues where the Torah readings for the week are divided between the Friday evening and Saturday morning services. Some congregations have separate rules for bat mitzvah girls relating to the Torah reading. Be certain to check with your rabbi if your daughter would like to read from the Torah.

Typically, the Friday evening service is followed by an *oneg Shabbat* at the synagogue for the entire congregation. This includes desserts, fruit display, coffee, tea and soft drinks. The Friday evening service with a Bat Mitzvah ceremony and an *oneg shabbat* usually runs from about 8:30–10:30 P.M.

Mincha and Havdalah

Over a period of time, holding prayer services three times daily became a fixed Jewish practice. The schedule of prayer services corresponds to the prescribed order of offerings which were made in the days of the Temple. When the Temple was no longer standing and the Jews were dispersed, leaders of the Jewish community determined that communal prayer was an appropriate substitute for these earlier sacrifices. In fact, the Hebrew word, *Mincha,* means present or offering, reflecting how this service would now take the place of sacrifices which formerly were made at that time of day. This is the origin of *Mincha,* the afternoon service.

Mincha occurs before sunset, around 4:30 P.M., in the winter, and 7:30 P.M., in the spring through fall months, when the days are longer. Typically, the Torah is read at this Shabbat afternoon service. It can be a very nice setting for a Bar/Bat Mitzvah ceremony. It could be a less demanding experience. Perhaps at this time your child might be given the opportunity for more personal or even creative participation.

The *Mincha* service can be followed directly by the traditional third meal, the *seudah shlishit,* sometimes known as *shalosh seudot.* On the Sabbath, from sundown Friday until sundown Saturday, it is customary to have three meals. The *seudah shlishit* is a simple meal served in the synagogue just before Shabbat concludes.

You may have heard the phrase, "a *Havdalah* Bar Mitzvah." Just as the beginning of Shabbat is ushered in with the lighting of candles, so does the ending of this day call for a special ritual, *Havdalah* which separates Shabbat from the work week. Often a Saturday afternoon Bar/Bat Mitzvah ceremony includes *Havdalah* along with the earlier *Mincha* service during which the Torah is read. Wherever you observe this *Havdalah* ceremony, whether it's at the synagogue or at home, it maintains a tone appropriate to the occasion. At the end of Shabbat, the lighting of the braided *Havdalah* candle with the accompanying blessings for wine, spices, and light, is a very moving moment. In this case, the candlelighting serves as an additional reminder of the beauty of the day, the Shabbat of your child's Bar/Bat Mitzvah.

If you are interested in having a Bar/Bat Mitzvah ceremony at a Saturday afternoon service, check first with your rabbi. While some may encourage or permit this, others may prefer that your child participate in the usually better attended services on Friday evening or Saturday morning.

It is possible to take part in both the Saturday morning service and the afternoon service on Shabbat. In this way, you can have an all-day experience, returning to the synagogue for *Mincha/Havdalah* and an evening celebration. The emotional pitch and religious connection is maintained throughout the day; the festivities keep the primary focus on communal worship and the synagogue.

Other Services: A Monday or Thursday Torah Service, Rosh Hodesh, a Festival

In some congregations, the Torah is read on Mondays and Thursdays, as well as at the regular Shabbat services. This tradition goes back to the days of the Temple when the Torah was read on market days—Mondays and Thursdays—so that all could hear the law. It may be possible for your child to be called up to the Torah as a Bar/Bat Mitzvah at one of these weekday services. This may be a good choice. When appropriate, some people plan a Bar/Bat Mitzvah on the Monday of a secular holiday such as Memorial Day or Labor Day. A child we know had a Bar Mitzvah on December 25 when it fell on a Thursday. A Monday or Thursday ceremony can be particularly desirable if you have invited guests who are *Shomer Shabbat.* Strictly observant Jews will not travel by car on Friday night or Saturday and so a weekday observance is easier for them to attend. Also, on Monday or Thursday the regular congregation may be small, with those present primarily your own guests. In this smaller congregation a child with learning limitations may feel more comfortable having his bar/bat mitzvah. On the other hand, an extremely capable and knowledge-able child may be allowed to lead more of the service at this time than he might be permitted to do on Saturday morning.

Some synagogues hold services on *Rosh Hodesh,* which is the first day of a new Hebrew month. Many congregations have services on the mornings of the Jewish festivals: *Sukkot, Pesach,* and *Shavuot* when the Torah customarily is read. It may be possible to schedule a Bar/Bat Mitzvah ceremony at these times if this is a good alternative for you and if it meets with the approval of your congregation. Whatever you plan, remember that a Bar/Bat Mitzvah is not a strictly personal event. It is a ritual made possible by a fully developed Jewish community, and you must place your celebration in the context of what is appropriate within your congregation.

NOTES:

Preparing
Your Child

Preparing Your Child

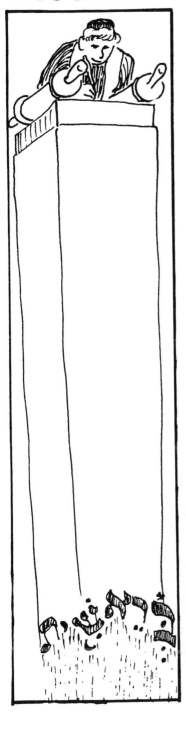

Basic Training

A course of study will prepare your youngster for the Bar/Bat Mitzvah ceremony. The child's role in the service depends on his skills and interest and the customs of the congregation. The child usually is called upon to read from the Torah, to chant the *Haftarah,* and perhaps to lead parts of the *Shabbat* morning service. Public reading of the Torah is a fundamental part of the synagogue service. A different portion is read on each *Shabbat* in the yearly cycle. Therefore, your child's Bar/Bat Mitzvah date will have a specific Torah portion and an accompanying *Haftarah* from the prophets.

Arrangements for Bar/Bat Mitzvah training can be made through the synagogue. Sometimes, all pre-Bar/Bat Mitzvah children are taught as a group, so that they can gain the general skills required for this occasion. Together they can learn the blessings said when one is called up to the Torah for an *aliyah* and those said before and after chanting the *Haftarah.* Basic synagogue skills can also be taught at this time: the use of the *tallit, tefillin;* the blowing of a *shofar;* how to lift and dress the Torah, and other Jewish practices.

As the child prepares for his Bar/Bat Mitzvah, he may be taught the distinctive *trope* for the Torah and the one for the *Haftarah.* Learning to read *trope* instead of simply memorizing the portion will enable your child to use that skill in years to come. The process is like learning to read music. Understanding the melodic notation will help your child master his portion and feel comfortable and secure when delivering it in public.

35

Individualized Tutoring

In addition, an individualized tutoring program will prepare each child for his specific role before the congregation on his Bar/Bat Mitzvah date. A cantor, who has trained over a thousand students, spends four to six months with each one. Of course, your child's preparation schedule will depend on the frequency of tutorial sessions, his prior Jewish education and what he will be doing on the day of his ceremony. This training may be provided by your congregation or you may have to hire a private tutor. The cantor, a religious school teacher, a capable post-Bar/Bat Mitzvah student, or someone else from the Jewish community can all be effective. A rare case is the parent or older sibling who is able and willing to tutor. This can work well if both can comfortably move to a teacher-student relationship.

Who would serve as a good role model for your child? With whom would he enjoy working? Of course, having a tutor from the synagogue has the added advantage of reinforcing your child's connection to this religious institution. Your major concern may be the location of the tutorial sessions: at home, at the synagogue, or elsewhere. Make certain that transportation arrangements are sufficiently convenient so that you do not resent the tutorial sessions. That would undermine your child's preparation and attitude. If you prefer to have someone come to your home, contact your synagogue, a local Jewish bookstore or Jewish newspaper to find a qualified traveling tutor. It is best to work out the cost of the tutorial sessions in advance as charges may vary widely.

There are two distinct forms of Hebrew pronunciation, *Ashkenazic* and *Sephardic*. *Ashkenazic* was originally used in Eastern Europe. During the Holocaust, most of the European Jews who prayed in *Ashkenazic* were exterminated by the Nazis. Despite this tragedy, this form of Hebrew still remains as the language of prayer in some congregations. The other pronunciation, *Sephardic,* originated in Spain and spread to North Africa and other resettlement areas after the Jews were expelled from Spain in 1492. Strengthened by being the Hebrew spoken in Israel today, the Sephardic pronunciation is the most commonly used. In *Sephardic,* the Hebrew letter *Taf* is pronounced like a "T," while, in *Ashkenazic,* it is said as an "S," as in *Shabbat* as compared to *Shabbos.* There are many other differences between these two forms of spoken Hebrew and your child should prepare using the pronunciation favored by your synagogue.

One can say the same written but unvoweled Hebrew word in a number of different ways. During the dispersion outside the land of Israel, the Jews lost their familiarity with the correct pronunciation of Hebrew texts. Only the learned were certain that they were reading and pronouncing the writings correctly. A system of vowels evolved in written Hebrew which clarifies pronunciation. With the passage of time, *trope* was developed in order to make it easier to remember and chant the words of the Torah and *Haftarah.* While the marks have not changed or shifted position over the years, there is flexibility in individual expression and interpretation. Before preparing your child, check with your synagogue to see what melodic forms are used in your congregation. If a melody has been passed down in your family, ask your rabbi if you may follow it during your child's ceremony. It should be noted that in some congregations, the Torah and *Haftarah* may be recited rather than chanted, then the issue of melodic notations will not apply. Many children have an easy time following the melodic notations when chanting Torah and *Haftarah.* Others find it more difficult. To help their children feel comfortable and confident, some parents have arranged for a brief series of voice lessons to help their child to hear and to follow the musical pitch. If this might be helpful to your bar/bat mitzvah student, check whether such instruction is available locally. Then, you can suggest this possibility and see if your child is at all interested.

Study Aids

The Torah has been copied meticulously in hand-lettered Hebrew by learned scribes. It has remained unchanged, without vowel or *trope* signs, for thousands of years until today. In studying the Bar/Bat Mitzvah portion, your child will be helped by using a *Tikkun.* A *Tikkun* is a book which contains one column with a copy of the hand-lettered Torah printed exactly as it looks on the *Sefer Torah* in your synagogue ark. On the adjacent column is the identical passage written in modern Hebrew print with markings indicating vowel sounds and melodic patterns. While your child will be aided by practicing the Torah portion with the *Tikkun,* he will not be allowed to use it on the *bimah.* When reading his portion at the Bar/Bat Mitzvah, your child will be in front of the congregation, pointing with a *yad,* chanting from the *Sefer Torah* written in the traditional hand-lettered manner.

Shilo Publishing House, Inc. offers study aids for the individual child's Bar/Bat Mitzvah preparation. It distributes four separate series which all contain the *Maftir, Haftarah,* and their accompanying blessings. The series of study aids are available as a booklet, book, record, or cassette. There is one for each week of the annual Torah-reading cycle. The booklets, called *"Hamaftir"* are numbered and named for the Torah portion of the week. Booklet #3, for example, refers to the third week in the yearly cycle and is also identified by the traditional name of the portion, *"Lech Lecha."* These booklets are printed with vowels and melodic markings. They also contain the *Haftarah* translation and instructions and prayers for the use of *tefillin.*

בְּרֵאשִׁית בָּרָא אֱלֹהִים אֵת הַשָּׁמַיִם וְאֵת הָאָרֶץ׃ וְהָאָרֶץ
הָיְתָה תֹהוּ וָבֹהוּ וְחֹשֶׁךְ עַל־פְּנֵי תְהוֹם וְרוּחַ אֱלֹהִים
מְרַחֶפֶת עַל־פְּנֵי הַמָּיִם׃ וַיֹּאמֶר אֱלֹהִים יְהִי אוֹר וַיְהִי־
אוֹר׃ וַיַּרְא אֱלֹהִים אֶת־הָאוֹר כִּי־טוֹב וַיַּבְדֵּל אֱלֹהִים בֵּין
הָאוֹר וּבֵין הַחֹשֶׁךְ׃ וַיִּקְרָא אֱלֹהִים ׀ לָאוֹר יוֹם וְלַחֹשֶׁךְ
קָרָא לָיְלָה וַיְהִי־עֶרֶב וַיְהִי־בֹקֶר יוֹם אֶחָד׃ פ

וַיֹּאמֶר אֱלֹהִים יְהִי רָקִיעַ בְּתוֹךְ הַמָּיִם וִיהִי מַבְדִּיל בֵּן
מַיִם לָמָיִם׃ וַיַּעַשׂ אֱלֹהִים אֶת־הָרָקִיעַ וַיַּבְדֵּל בֵּין הַמַּיִם
אֲשֶׁר מִתַּחַת לָרָקִיעַ וּבֵין הַמַּיִם אֲשֶׁר מֵעַל לָרָקִיעַ וַיְהִי־
כֵן׃ וַיִּקְרָא אֱלֹהִים לָרָקִיעַ שָׁמָיִם וַיְהִי־עֶרֶב וַיְהִי־בֹקֶר
יוֹם שֵׁנִי׃ פ

וַיֹּאמֶר אֱלֹהִים יִקָּווּ הַמַּיִם מִתַּחַת הַשָּׁמַיִם אֶל־מָקוֹם אֶחָד
וְתֵרָאֶה הַיַּבָּשָׁה וַיְהִי־כֵן׃ וַיִּקְרָא אֱלֹהִים ׀ לַיַּבָּשָׁה אֶרֶץ
וּלְמִקְוֵה הַמַּיִם קָרָא יַמִּים וַיַּרְא אֱלֹהִים כִּי־טוֹב׃ וַיֹּאמֶר
אֱלֹהִים תַּדְשֵׁא הָאָרֶץ דֶּשֶׁא עֵשֶׂב מַזְרִיעַ זֶרַע עֵץ פְּרִי
עֹשֶׂה פְּרִי לְמִינוֹ אֲשֶׁר זַרְעוֹ־בוֹ עַל־הָאָרֶץ וַיְהִי־כֵן׃
וַתּוֹצֵא הָאָרֶץ דֶּשֶׁא עֵשֶׂב מַזְרִיעַ זֶרַע לְמִינֵהוּ וְעֵץ עֹשֶׂה־
פְּרִי אֲשֶׁר זַרְעוֹ־בוֹ לְמִינֵהוּ וַיַּרְא אֱלֹהִים כִּי־טוֹב׃ וַיְהִי־
עֶרֶב וַיְהִי־בֹקֶר יוֹם שְׁלִישִׁי׃ פ

וַיֹּאמֶר אֱלֹהִים יְהִי מְאֹרֹת בִּרְקִיעַ הַשָּׁמַיִם לְהַבְדִּיל בֵּין
הַיּוֹם וּבֵין הַלָּיְלָה וְהָיוּ לְאֹתֹת וּלְמוֹעֲדִים וּלְיָמִים וְשָׁנִים׃
וְהָיוּ לִמְאוֹרֹת בִּרְקִיעַ הַשָּׁמַיִם לְהָאִיר עַל־הָאָרֶץ וַיְהִי־
כֵן׃ וַיַּעַשׂ אֱלֹהִים אֶת־שְׁנֵי הַמְּאֹרֹת הַגְּדֹלִים אֶת־הַמָּאוֹר
הַגָּדֹל לְמֶמְשֶׁלֶת הַיּוֹם וְאֶת־הַמָּאוֹר הַקָּטֹן לְמֶמְשֶׁלֶת
הַלַּיְלָה וְאֵת הַכּוֹכָבִים׃ וַיִּתֵּן אֹתָם אֱלֹהִים בִּרְקִיעַ
הַשָּׁמָיִם לְהָאִיר עַל־הָאָרֶץ׃ וְלִמְשֹׁל בַּיּוֹם וּבַלַּיְלָה
וּלֲהַבְדִּיל בֵּין הָאוֹר וּבֵין הַחֹשֶׁךְ וַיַּרְא אֱלֹהִים כִּי־טוֹב׃
וַיְהִי־עֶרֶב וַיְהִי־בֹקֶר יוֹם רְבִיעִי׃ פ

וַיֹּאמֶר אֱלֹהִים יִשְׁרְצוּ הַמַּיִם שֶׁרֶץ נֶפֶשׁ חַיָּה וְעוֹף יְעוֹפֵף
עַל־הָאָרֶץ עַל־פְּנֵי רְקִיעַ הַשָּׁמָיִם׃ וַיִּבְרָא אֱלֹהִים אֶת־
הַתַּנִּינִם הַגְּדֹלִים וְאֵת כָּל־נֶפֶשׁ הַחַיָּה ׀ הָרֹמֶשֶׂת אֲשֶׁר
שָׁרְצוּ הַמַּיִם לְמִינֵהֶם וְאֵת כָּל־עוֹף כָּנָף לְמִינֵהוּ וַיַּרְא
אֱלֹהִים כִּי־טוֹב׃ וַיְבָרֶךְ אֹתָם אֱלֹהִים לֵאמֹר פְּרוּ וּרְבוּ
וּמִלְאוּ אֶת־הַמַּיִם בַּיַּמִּים וְהָעוֹף יִרֶב בָּאָרֶץ׃ וַיְהִי־עֶרֶב
וַיְהִי־בֹקֶר יוֹם חֲמִישִׁי׃ פ

וַיֹּאמֶר אֱלֹהִים תּוֹצֵא הָאָרֶץ נֶפֶשׁ חַיָּה לְמִינָהּ בְּהֵמָה
וָרֶמֶשׂ וְחַיְתוֹ־אֶרֶץ לְמִינָהּ וַיְהִי־כֵן׃ וַיַּעַשׂ אֱלֹהִים אֶת־
חַת הָאָרֶץ לְמִינָהּ וְאֶת־הַבְּהֵמָה לְמִינָהּ

בראשית ברא אלהים את השמים ואת הארץ
והארץ היתה תהו ובהו וחשך על פני תהום ורוח
אלהים מרחפת על פני המים ויאמר אלהים יהי
אור ויהי אור וירא אלהים את האור כי טוב
ויבדל אלהים בין האור ובין החשך ויקרא
אלהים לאור יום ולחשך קרא לילה ויהי ערב
ויהי בקר יום אחד

ויאמר אלהים יהי רקיע בתוך המים ויהי מבדיל
בין מים למים ויעש אלהים את הרקיע ויבדל
בין המים אשר מתחת לרקיע ובין המים אשר
מעל לרקיע ויהי כן ויקרא אלהים לרקיע שמים
ויהי ערב ויהי בקר יום שני

ויאמר אלהים יקוו המים מתחת השמים אל
מקום אחד ותראה היבשה ויהי כן ויקרא אלהים
ליבשה ארץ ולמקוה המים קרא ימים וירא
אלהים כי טוב ויאמר אלהים תדשא הארץ
דשא עשב מזריע זרע עץ פרי עשה פרי למינו
אשר זרעו בו על הארץ ויהי כן ותוצא הארץ
דשא עשב מזריע זרע למינהו ועץ עשה פרי
אשר זרעו בו למינהו וירא אלהים כי טוב ויהי
ערב ויהי בקר יום שלישי

ויאמר אלהים יהי מארת ברקיע השמים להבדיל
בין היום ובין הלילה והיו לאתת ולמועדים ולימים
ושנים והיו למאורת ברקיע השמים להאיר על
הארץ ויהי כן ויעש אלהים את שני המארת
הגדלים את המאור הגדל לממשלת היום ואת
המאור הקטן לממשלת הלילה ואת הכוכבים
ויתן אתם אלהים ברקיע השמים להאיר על
הארץ ולמשל ביום ובלילה ולהבדיל בין האור
ובין החשך וירא אלהים כי טוב ויהי ערב ויהי
בקר יום רביעי

ויאמר אלהים ישרצו המים שרץ נפש חיה
ועוף יעופף על הארץ על פני רקיע השמים
ויברא אלהים את התנינם הגדלים ואת כל נפש
החיה הרמשת אשר שרצו המים למינהם ואת
כל עוף כנף למינהו וירא אלהים כי טוב ויברך
אתם אלהים לאמר פרו ורבו ומלאו את המים
בימים והעוף ירב בארץ ויהי ערב ויהי בקר
יום חמישי

ויאמר אלהים תוצא הארץ נפש חיה למינה
בהמה ורמש וחיתו ארץ למינה ויהי כן ויעש
אלהים את חית הארץ למינה ואת הבהמה למינה

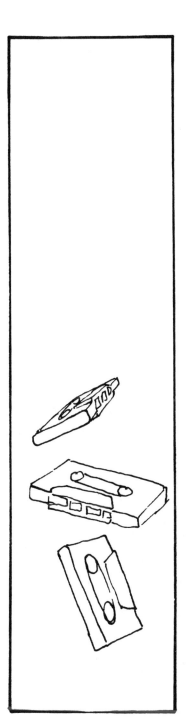

Shilo also publishes a second series called *My Bar Mitzvah Book,* which includes everything in *"Hamaftir,"* plus additional articles on the Torah, Ten Commandments, Prophets, and a discussion of the teachings of that week's *Haftarah.* This supplemental information may be of interest to your child. Their records and cassettes cover each week of the Jewish calendar year. The tapes use *Sephardic* pronunciation while the records can be obtained with either *Sephardic* or *Ashkenazic* Hebrew. The Shilo series can be found in a local Jewish bookstore, perhaps your synagogue shop, or they can be ordered directly from Shilo Publishing House, Inc., 73 Canal Street, New York, NY 10002, (212) 925-3468.

The Union of American Hebrew Congregations (UAHC) publication catalogue offers pamphlets for each Torah and *Haftarah* portion with cantillation and the appropriate blessings. In addition to these fifty-four pamphlets, UAHC has the *Haftarah* for special days such as *Pesach, Yom HaShoah* and *Sukkot.* To make the Bar/Bat Mitzvah a total Jewish educational experience, these pamphlets include Jewish history, commentaries, *midrash* and contemporary applications of each portion to modern Jewish life. To order these, call (212) 249-0100 or FAX (212) 570-0895.

If you own a computer, Davka Corporation provides materials for training your child. Founded in 1982, it is the largest supplier of Hebrew and Judaic software for IBM, Apple and Macintosh. You can order the Torah and *Haftarah* blessings as well as your child's specific *Haftarah* portion. For more information, contact Davka at: (800) 621-8227, (312) 465-4070 or FAX (312) 262-9298.

Lev Software in Florida also provides excellent Bar/Bat Mitzvah preparation. Their software requires an IBM compatible or a Macintosh with a special package to integrate with IBM. Lev features full color graphics. Their programs can teach your child to read and write Hebrew using their three different fonts for print, script, or Torah script. One program, "Haftutor", includes all 54 Torah and Haftarah portions as well as the blessings. The Lev design allows the computer to make the vowels disappear and reappear, play in every musical key, play at a comfortable tempo, point to every syllable, transliterate Hebrew into English and Russian, or print out any screen page. Call them at (800) 776-6538 for more information about all their Bar/Bat Mitzvah related products.

Another, more informal, learning aid is a cassette prepared by your child's tutor. The Bar/Bat Mitzvah blessings and readings can be recorded phrase by phrase with a space for repetition in between. In this way, the student can copy and practice on his own whenever he wishes. All of these study aids can assist the Bar/Bat Mitzvah student in his preparation.

D'Rash, Bar/Bat Mitzvah Speech, Personal Prayer

There are many ways in which your child may expand his part in the service. In medieval Germany it was common for a child to give a public discourse to demonstrate his learning. These words of Torah were often given at the feast following the ceremony itself, thus helping to keep a religious tone at the celebration. From this stems the contemporary practices of having a child deliver a *d'var Torah*, describe the message of his *Haftarah*, make a speech and say a prayer before the Ark. If your child is preparing for one of these, he can be assisted by his tutor or rabbi. Here are guidelines for these presentations.

In giving a speech about his Torah or *Haftarah* portion, a child should be confident that he understands what he is saying and that the message he is giving is clear to the listeners. A junior high-school-age child may find writing difficult. The parent or tutor can help the child develop his thoughts by talking with the child and then typing or writing down his ideas so he can review and polish his presentation. We have been to a service where a child put a lot of effort into his remarks, but it was lost through a poor delivery. Public speakers avoid mumbling, speaking too softly or too quickly. Some adult supervision helps assure that the speech will be organized, of reasonable length, and well delivered. If you have a video camera, you may want to tape your child's speech and play it back to him for improvements.

If the child, and perhaps the parents, choose to say a personal prayer before the congregation, these should reflect their own feelings and sense of gratitude. Too much religious fervor, cute comments, memories of the child's day of birth may not be suitable for this occasion. Here are some suggestions for composing such a prayer:[1]

---

1. Stanley Rabinowitz, *Prayers for the Bar Mitzvah Child* (Washington, D.C.: Adas Israel Congregation).

- The prayer the child chooses may express a feeling of gratitude upon reaching this milestone in life.
- A child may ask for God's blessings on his family and teachers for having guided him and prepared him for this occasion.
- The child may wish to express aspirations for his future as well as hopes for the welfare of the Jewish people.
- The child may wish to pledge that he will continue studying and will remain devoted to the ideals of his faith.

Many rabbis arrange for a meeting with the Bar/Bat Mitzvah and his parents before the ceremony. In any event, you may wish to give the rabbi some background material about your child and family. You may outline some of your child's interests and/or accomplishments. There is always something interesting to say. You may also include information about special relatives and those who have traveled great distances to attend. This will give the rabbi specifics for the personal remarks that he will undoubtedly direct to your child on the Bar/Bat Mitzvah day.

Understanding the Synagogue Service

To give needed support to your child, the immediate family should also be familiar with the service at which the Bar Mitzvah is being held. If you do not ordinarily attend services at your synagogue, you should make a point of going regularly before your Bar/Bat Mitzvah. The service may seem foreign or unfamiliar, or even without much meaning to you. Those feelings can be overcome by attendance, participation, or guidance from synagogue members who attend regularly. Here is some vocabulary for the Saturday morning service.

SHEMA: It is one of the oldest and most significant Jewish prayers, proclaiming God's power, nearness and unity. It begins "Hear, O Israel, the Lord is Our God, the Lord is One."

AMIDAH: Central to every Jewish service is this prayer, said while standing. It contains varying blessings of praise, petition and gratitude.

KADDISH: The kaddish, the most famous one of which is the mourners' kaddish, is used to separate sections of a service. It uses many adjectives to praise God, to proclaim his sovereignty, and to affirm our faith in God at all times.

HALLEL: These psalms of praise are added to the regular service on special days. They are recited at the beginning of a new month, at *Pesach, Shavuot,* and *Sukkot,* and at *Chanukah.*

There are many ways to improve one's understanding of the Saturday morning service. You can attend a learners' minyan. This introductory service is a popular offering at many congregations. It moves slowly; page numbers are called frequently; Hebrew reading is done phonetically; explanations are given for the meaning of prayers. If your congregation does not hold such a learners service, you might want to suggest that they add it to their schedule. In addition, Hebrew classes are available in most communities. If you study introductory or prayer book Hebrew, it will help you unlock the meaning of the service. In addition, various congregations throughout the country hold a one-day Hebrew Marathon to help adults make a breakthrough to Hebrew literacy. This successful program is based on word recognition and helps people overcome their anxieties. One can also find the Saturday morning service—its music and its ritual—on tapes and videocassettes. For example, the Federation of Jewish Men's Clubs has an 18 minute video explaining the parts of the Torah service. Any of these programs and materials can help you become more comfortable at services.

Tips for Success

Your child can benefit from a few words of advice about what to expect and how to behave throughout the ceremony. This is best discussed in a quiet moment. You may make the following suggestions, taking into consideration the customs of your particular congregation:

- Follow the service with an open book, participating in prayers and songs.
- Do not wave or signal friends and family from the bimah.
- Sit on the bimah in a dignified manner.
- Be prepared to shake hands with the rabbi, cantor, those presenting gifts (e.g., the Sisterhood president).

The Bar/Bat Mitzvah child will be the center of attention, somewhat overwhelmed at times, but in the back of his mind should be this parental encouragement on how to be friendly, composed, and polite at this, his big moment.

About three weeks before the Bar/Bat Mitzvah date, hold at least one dress rehearsal in the sanctuary. This will help set your child at ease as he practices where to stand, how to face the open Ark, volume levels (with a microphone, if one is used), and whatever else needs to be reviewed. If possible, he should practice chanting his portion from the *Sefer Torah* from which he will be reading at the ceremony. Reassure your child that he will do well. If necessary, remind him that the quality of his chanting voice is not significant. This is a time when some children's voices may be changing and others are simply not that musical. Musical ability is not the issue. The Bar/Bat Mitzvah ceremony marks the culmination of a period of Jewish study with a public religious ceremony. It is this, not the voice, that is important. A reassuring call from the tutor can give an added psychological boost, sometimes very necessary in these last days before the Bar/Bat Mitzvah.

Clearly, a Bar/Bat Mitzvah is an important emotional event for the child and his family. Understandably, there is anxiety beforehand, rejoicing as the ceremony takes place, and often a post-Bar/Bat Mitzvah letdown when all the excitement is over. The usual little sports accidents take on more meaning and may occur more frequently in the weeks before the Bar/Bat Mitzvah. Active young teenagers are often in slings and casts, and this time is no exception. One Bar Mitzvah boy we know was so aware of his parents' concerns about his health that it led him to write a very amusing short story:

> "Irving, now that Joel is in perfect condition, how are we going to keep him this way for his Bar Mitzvah? We can't have him go up to the *bimah* with a broken leg or stitches over his eyes," Miriam said.
> "Yes, I know, Miriam. With his past record, he will have something wrong with him, if we don't do something. Why, just last month, he had a broken toe, and he had a terrible case of poison ivy, he stepped on a nail, and got bitten by a rabbit. What more could happen?" Irving said.

The story goes on to describe how Joel was put to bed for two weeks prior to his Bar Mitzvah. Even then, something happened. The story ends when:

> Miriam realized, at last, that Joel wouldn't be his real self, without *some*thing being wrong with him.[2]

If your plans are set ahead of time, you can remain cheerful even when the unexpected occurs at the last moment. Tension is common the week before the big event. Your child will be sensitive to any anxiety his parents express. Guest lists, family personalities, and seating plans may demand your attention. Don't confuse your child by losing sight of the fact that the religious ceremony is the heart of the Bar/Bat Mitzvah experience.

Your twelve- or thirteen-year-old may have waves of cheerful anticipation, alternating with despair about his ability to uphold the central role in this special occasion. Just prior to her Friday night ceremony, one young girl told her rabbi, "I don't think I can do it. I'm going to faint." He reassured her by suggesting that she wait until after the service! Feelings of this sort are normal. So much rests on your child's shoulders as he is called to stand alone before the entire congregation. Therefore, your child needs to be well prepared and given much parental support. Take time to listen to your child's concerns and express your confidence in his ability to do a fine job. The personal sense of achievement and joy of completion come from having mastered a difficult task. With this feeling of accomplishment, the Bar/Bat Mitzvah ceremony will mark a meaningful point in your child's life.

---

2. David Pomerantz, "The Bar Mitzvah Boy," *Reflections,* Vol. 3 (Rockville, Md., 1978).

The Importance of a Jewish Education

As a Bar/Bat Mitzvah, your child will be called up to the Torah. Several years of Jewish education should precede this ceremony, providing a foundation for his identity. In these early years, the youngster is introduced to the joys of Judaism, its holiday cycle, enduring values and unique history. Ongoing study has always been important to Jews who take to heart the message of Hillel who said: "Do not say 'when I shall have leisure I shall study' for you may never have leisure." (*Pirke Avot* Chapter II, 5). While the Bar/Bat Mitzvah is an occasion for joy, it can be a time for concern if your child feels that he is now finished with his Jewish education. You would not allow your child to leave school after seventh grade, ignorant of science, literature, history and higher math. Dennis Prager and Joseph Telushkin have observed:

> Just as a poor education in chemistry will produce poor chemists or no chemists, so a poor Jewish education will produce poor Jews or no Jews; and the chances of alienation from Jewish identity increase even more in the proportion that secular education surpasses in time and quality Jewish education.[3]

What can be done? Seeking to offer intensive Jewish education, many communities support Jewish day schools which treat Judaic and general studies with equal seriousness. In addition, many teenagers take part in continuing synagogue programs. At the high school level, they grapple with the deeper philosophic issues that are at the heart of Biblical and prophetic writings. Books, such as Rabbi Roland Gittelson's *How Do I Decide?*, challenge students to use insights of Judaism to help clarify their personal values. Topics are relevant to teen-agers: substance abuse, AIDS, abortion, divorce. In addition to continued

3. *Nine Questions People Ask About Judaism* (Simon and Schuster, New York, 1981), p. 136.

schooling, being connected to a Jewish youth group offers an important sense of belonging to the adolescent. Study groups, seminars, social action projects, pizza nights with the rabbi may blur the lines between informal and formal instruction. Different programs work for different teen-agers to maintain their interest and involvement.

Many principals are now actively encouraging, if not insisting, that parents participate actively in their children's education. The wrong message is given if the parents put full responsibility on the school and do not reinforce these values at home. Parents are encouraged to be role models who show that Jewish learning is a continuing partnership and a lifelong process. To work towards these goals, family education programs such as holiday workshops, joint parent-child activities, and seminars for Bar/Bat Mitzvah parents, are held at the synagogue. Whatever the depth of your commitment, we urge you, as parents, to give your children the best Jewish education possible.

One might say that in his studies, the Bar/Bat Mitzvah child is in a position similar to a contractor who worked many years for a large construction company. One day, he was given plans to build a lovely home in a nice residential area. He was told to spare no expense. As the work progressed, the contractor thought to himself, "Who would know if I don't use the most expensive and best materials and labor? Outwardly, the house will look the same." He began to substitute cheap, poor quality materials and labor, pocketing the difference as his gain. Shortly after the house was completed, a reception was held to celebrate the occasion. The chairman of the board surprised the contractor by presenting him with the keys to the house as a gift. It was to be a token of their esteem for his long and high-quality service. In the years that followed, the contractor never ceased to regret the way that he had cheated, "If only I had known that I was building the house for myself!"[4] So it is with the Bar/Bat Mitzvah. The child may fulfill his potential and meet his obligations or do less and ultimately weaken himself and the community. Many hopes rest on his shoulders on his Bar/Bat Mitzvah day as the influence of the past and the expectations for the future join together in sharp focus.

4. Morris Mandel, *Thirteen: A Teenage Guide to Judaism* (New York: Jonathan David Publishers, 1961), pp. 26–27.

Education for the Child with Special Needs

The Jewish community strives to offer a Jewish education to all its members. No child should be denied religious training because he or she cannot function successfully in a regular school setting. Most large cities and many smaller ones offer support for children with physical, behavioral, learning or other developmental disabilities. These services can be provided within the framework of a synagogue school or day school.

The community approach can be very effective in aiding students with unique learning needs. The Jewish community of greater Washington, D.C. provides a well-known and respected model where Jewish children, from those with minimal difficulties to others with severe disabilities, can be included in the mainstream of Jewish life. Their Board of Jewish Education (BJE) provides training for congregational and day schools to help them accommodate students with special learning needs. For children who require non-intensive and individualized educational support, the Jewish Community Center offers a self-contained program. Instructional strategies developed for secular special education are being adapted for use in synagogues and day schools.

"Experiencing a Bar/Bat Mitzvah can be the single most normalizing experience in a Jewish child's life" states Sara Rubinow Simon, Director, Special Needs Department, BJE of Greater Washington. Communities across North America have increasingly witnessed the Bar/Bat Mitzvah ceremonies of young people with varying disabilities. These include sign language interpretation of services by children who are deaf and services of modified length and content for people who are mentally retarded. Ramps and elevators offer improved accessibility. Bar/Bat Mitzvah need not be limited to age thirteen. Therefore, persons with special needs may hold their ceremony at a later date. In fact, adults with severe disabilities, who never had the opportunity, are now involved in their own Bar/Bat Mitzvah preparation. To reach this milestone, regardless of age, is most meaningful for these individuals and their families.

A Bar/Bat Mitzvah child may want to consider sharing his Bar/Bat Mitzvah date with someone who has special needs. Both participate to the extent of their abilities. The joint ceremony benefits the individuals involved as well as the community by demonstrating that whatever one's capacities, one can experience this rite of passage.

More and more is being done to assist the Jewish child with special needs. Guides, such as United Synagogue's *My Child is Different* by Rabbi Robert Layman, offer perspective to parents. To learn more about Washington's approach to special needs, contact Sara Rubinow Simon, BJE, 11710 Hunters Lane, Rockville, MD 20852 (301) 984-4455 or Sara Portman Milner, JCC, 6125 Montrose Road, Rockville, MD 20852 (301) 881-0100 or (301) 881-0012, TDD. For local assistance, turn to sources in your own community. In addition, the Jewish Education Service of North America, 730 Broadway, New York, NY 10003, (212) 529-2000 publishes a national directory of programs in different communities. They also can provide individual consultative support.

Courtesy of Washington's BJE, here are points to consider when preparing a special needs child for a Bar/Bat Mitzvah:

Preparation

1. Is my child self-motivated?
2. Is s/he anxiously awaiting Bar/Bat Mitzvah or just anxious?
3. Does my child work well one-on-one?
4. Can my child read Hebrew or does s/he have the potential for learning Hebrew?
5. Does my child learn better auditorially or visually?
6. Would my child do better with frequent, short lessons or longer lessons once a week?
7. What are my child's expectations?

Selection of Tutor

1. Does this person understand my child's strengths and limitations?
2. Can the tutor be flexible in teaching methods?
3. Is the tutor familiar with the form of the service in my congregation?

Selection of Date and Time

1. Can my child sit through a service?
2. Is my child able to stand up in front of a large number of people, particularly strangers?
3. If my child is capable of learning a Haftarah, should I look for a week that has a shorter Haftarah selection?

4. Would my synagogue permit a Bar/Bat Mitzvah at another time, i.e. Rosh Hodesh, Monday or Thursday morning, afternoon-evening service?
5. What other responsibilities can my child take in the service, i.e. Sh'ma, Ain Kelohanu, readings in English, opening/closing of the Ark, wrapping Torah, etc.?
6. What options does my congregation offer?

Creative Bar/Bat Mitzvah Courses of Study

Recognizing the importance of the Bar/Bat Mitzvah year, many educators have designed programs for this age group. By this time, the child is expected to know the basic vocabulary of Jewish life. When a congregation offers the child the opportunity to celebrate a Bar/Bat Mitzvah, it attests to his knowledge and commitment as a new member of the adult Jewish community. We know of some schools who feel that their students should understand today's multifaceted Jewish life. To enrich their program, they went beyond the school walls to introduce students to various persons who reflect their Jewishness in their everyday work: a cantor, a kosher butcher, a UJA administrator, a Jewish funeral director, and others. Creative programs for Bar/Bat Mitzvah students are being developed by Jewish educators in Israel and the United States.

Many congregations run a series of classes for Bar/Bat Mitzvah parents. Not only does this provide adult education, but also it serves a social purpose bringing together a group of adults with common interests. If your congregation does not offer such courses, you may want to suggest that they do.

The Jewish Home
Transmitting Jewish Values

The individual Jewish home is the critical link in Jewish survival. In the home, children can experience firsthand the rhythm of the Jewish year—its holidays and celebrations. There parents can convey the joy of being Jewish. As parents, we try to pass on to our children Jewish values and a sense of identity with our people. There are many possible steps to take to enhance your home Jewishly such as: lighting candles on Friday night, collecting Jewish books, building a sukkah in your backyard, celebrating Chanukah with games and delicious latkes. Holidays invite family participation. You can get creative ideas for celebrating by checking *The Jewish Catalog* or *The Jewish Holidays* and other current books which describe traditions, crafts and foods customary for each holiday.

One kibbutz north of Haifa suggests that parents along with their children be responsible for thirteen *mitzvot* during the course of the year preceding the Bar/Bat Mitzvah. This could include visiting the sick, feeding the hungry or other creative projects. Parental participation is important as children prepare for coming of age by taking on adult responsibilities.

Many adults are involved in study groups so they can learn more about their Jewish heritage. Torah, Jewish medical ethics, *Pirke Avot*, Jewish history, Israeli literature or films are possible areas of study. Very often these groups meet in a participant's home with members taking turns hosting and leading. We know a growing number of families who regularly study Jewish texts at the Friday night dinner table. Each week the discussion focuses on a specific idea such as the weekly Torah portion, sibling rivalry, or cruelty to animals. Two books which will help you get started are David Epstein and Suzanne Stutman's *Torah With Love* and Joseph Telushkin's *Jewish Literacy*. Epstein and Stutman's book will tell you how to begin this process no matter what the level of your Jewish background. Telushkin's book will give you 364 different topics to discuss at your table. In addition, many commentaries are available in English making it easy for a parent to lead a discussion involving children of all ages. By elevating your table talk, you will build everyone's knowledge of Jewish history, religion and values. Here parents can set an important example to influence their children where they show that the insights of Jewish texts are relevant to everyday life.

Suggestions for Those Starting Late

There are times when a child has not been fortunate enough to have had a good Jewish background. In some families the parents do not assume the responsibility for giving their children a Jewish education. Despite this, the children, without parental guidance or pressure, have themselves sought to affirm their Jewish identity. They became conscientiously involved in Judaic studies, even motivating their parents to join a synagogue. When the impetus to become a Bar or Bat Mitzvah comes from a committed child, the parents should be sensitive to the child's desires to identify with his people and should encourage him to reach this goal.

Sometimes, approaching age thirteen, a child from an intermarriage may decide he wants to be part of the Jewish people and to prepare for a Bar or Bat Mitzvah. If the family can agree and the synagogue can support the idea, this can happen. If the mother is the non-Jewish parent, conversion for the child may be necessary.

The requirements for becoming a Bar/Bat Mitzvah vary from synagogue to synagogue. Many congregations require that a child attend religious school for a prescribed number of years. Hence, some children starting late may have a Bar/Bat

Mitzvah when they are fourteen or even older. However, we know an Orthodox congregation where the rabbi, following the legal definition of a Bar Mitzvah, accepts as a Bar Mitzvah a boy who is thirteen and one day and can recite the blessings before and after the Torah reading. While he accepts the traditional definition of Bar Mitzvah, he feels it belittles the significance of the occasion and does not advocate this approach.

NOTES:

Sharing
the Honors

Sharing
the Honors

The religious service is the heart of the bar/bat mitzvah experience. Here your child demonstrates that he is coming of age as an identified Jew. The rituals of the day show that adult Jews take seriously their connections to Jewish traditions. Their example will help the bar/bat mitzvah child and his friends to see that Jewish involvement is a lifelong commitment.

Being called to assist at a religious service is an honor, whether you open the ark, chant the Torah blessings or lift the Torah. It is customary to call individuals from the congregation to participate in the service. Often, the bar/bat mitzvah family may designate who will receive these honors. Check with your congregational leaders to see if women may receive the same honors as men. You should also ask if there are dress requirements for those participating in the service. Then, be sure to prepare your guests so that they know what to expect and what to do when called for their honor.

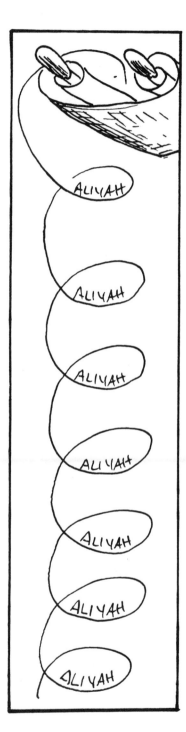

Aliyah—Being Called to the Torah

Being called to recite the blessings before and after the Torah is read is called an *aliyah*. It is a great privilege. One goes up literally as one ascends the *bimah* where the Torah is read and one goes up in a spiritual sense by participating in this ritual. The Hebrew word *aliyah* is also used to refer to moving to Israel, which is seen as a spiritual uplifting. According to tradition, there are seven *aliyot* and a *maftir* or concluding honor at a Saturday morning service. Maintaining the link between the Torah portion and the prophetic readings which follow, the *maftir* chants the concluding verses from the Torah reading with its accompanying blessings and then chants the *Haftarah*.

While the bar/bat mitzvah child is typically honored with *maftir*, the seven other *aliyot* may be yours to give as honors to your guests. Occasionally, there may be more *aliyot* if one further divides the portions. Or there may be more honors when an extra Torah scroll is used in the service. This happens on Shabbat of the new Hebrew month and certain holidays such as *Sukkot* and *Chanukah*. On the other hand, your synagogue may give out *aliyot* to other congregants so you are left with fewer than seven for your friends and family.

Furthermore, some rabbis follow a pattern in assigning *aliyot*. The first goes to a *Kohen* of priestly descent; the second to a *Levite* whose ancestors assisted the priests; and the rest to Israelites, other members of the congregation. The third and sixth are sometimes given to distinguished persons in the community, who are not *Kohanim* or *Levites*. According to differing traditions, the numerical position of an *aliyah* may be significant. While many accept that there is a scholar's *aliyah*, they do not necessarily agree which one it is. Check with the rabbi to learn the procedures for sharing the honors on your bar/bat mitzvah day.

In addition, be sure to let each guest know what is expected, so he will be prepared and comfortable when called for his honor. Usually, there is no rehearsal so your guests must rely on you for all needed information. Avoid the awkward moment when someone ascends the *bimah* and does not know what to do or say. Here are some suggestions to convey to your guests:

- Sit where you can easily get to the *bimah* when called.
- Be certain that men are wearing a *tallit* if customary in your synagogue.
- Listen for when you are called to the Torah. Sometimes you are called by your English name, but you may be called by your Hebrew name, for example, "Benyamin Meir ben Pinchas ha-Kohen" or "Natan ben Yaakov," or they may just call the number of the aliyah, *Ya-amod shishi* (sixth aliyah).
- Step up to the reading table and stand to the right of the Torah reader.
- Touch the fringe of your *tallit* or prayerbook to the spot in the Torah text indicated by the reader.
- Then recite the following blessings before reading the Torah:

ONE: You begin here:
Bor-chu et Ado-nai hamevorach.

בָּרְכוּ אֶת יְיָ הַמְבֹרָךְ.

Bless the Lord who is blessed.

TWO: The congregation makes the following response which you repeat:
Boruch Ado-nai hamevorach le-olam va-ed.

בָּרוּךְ יְיָ הַמְבֹרָךְ לְעוֹלָם וָעֶד.

Blessed is the Lord who is forever blessed.

THREE: You continue directly with the following blessing:
Boruch A-tah Ado-nai Elohenu Me-lech
Ha-olam a-sher boechar bo-nu me-call
ha-amim v'notan la-nu et Torah-to
Bouch A-tah Ado-nai no-ten ha-Torah.

בָּרוּךְ אַתָּה, יְיָ אֱלֹהֵינוּ, מֶלֶךְ הָעוֹלָם, אֲשֶׁר בָּחַר בָּנוּ מִכָּל
הָעַמִּים וְנָתַן לָנוּ אֶת תּוֹרָתוֹ. בָּרוּךְ אַתָּה, יְיָ, נוֹתֵן הַתּוֹרָה.

Blessed art Thou, Lord our God, Ruler of the universe, who has chosen us from among the nations and has given us His Torah. Blessed art Thou, Lord, who gives the Torah.

FOUR: After the Torah is read, touch the fringe of your tallit to the Torah as before and recite the concluding blessings:
Boruch A-tah Ado-nai Elo-henu Me-lech
Ha-olam a-sher no-tan la-nu Torat emet
v-cha-yay olam no-tah b'to-chenu
Boruch A-tah Ado-nai no-ten ha-Torah.

בָּרוּךְ אַתָּה, יְיָ אֱלֹהֵינוּ, מֶלֶךְ הָעוֹלָם, אֲשֶׁר נָתַן לָנוּ תּוֹרַת
אֱמֶת וְחַיֵּי עוֹלָם נָטַע בְּתוֹכֵנוּ. בָּרוּךְ אַתָּה, יְיָ, נוֹתֵן הַתּוֹרָה.

Blessed art Thou, Lord our God, Ruler of the universe, who has given us the Torah of truth and has implanted within us eternal life; Blessed art Thou, giver of the Torah.

You can photocopy these Torah blessings and mail the sheet to those honored with an *aliyah*. If you think it would be helpful, you can send a cassette tape with the recorded blessings as well.

It may be necessary to furnish the Hebrew names of those to be honored so that they may be called up accordingly. You may also need to know who is a *Kohen*, a *Levite*, and an *Israelite*. Have one copy of this list on the *bimah* and another in a capable usher's hands in the congregation to assure that the right person comes up at the specified time. Your guest may be new to your synagogue and may need assistance when his name is called, especially if it is called in Hebrew.

Grandparents and Their Participation

Grandparents stand as loving reminders of the continuity of the family. They offer a link to the past, while your child stands for the promise of the future. Grandparents and other older relatives should get special consideration at a Bar/Bat Mitzvah, for this is a ceremony which involves handing down the law, a generational concept. At one service, the maternal grandfather and paternal grandmother both chanted Torah portions before their grandson was called up as a Bar Mitzvah. We have also seen a grandfather, father, and son on the *bimah*, passing the Torah from one generation to another.

Grandparents of another faith have special needs at bar/bat mitzvah time. If the grandparents want to participate, there are many possible options depending on the customs of your congregation. It is important to check with your rabbi before assigning honors. We have seen non-Jewish grandparents proudly participate in the candle-lighting ceremony. Another nice touch is to have the grandparents provide a beautiful bouquet for the *bimah*. There are some non-Jewish grandparents who may not be happy with the bar/bat mizvah, a ceremony affirming Jewish identity. It is important to be sensitive to their needs as well.

Special Family Situations

There have been dramatic changes in the American family in the past two decades. A Jewish child may live in an interfaith household, a one parent household, or a blended, divorced or remarried family.

When a child from an interfaith home celebrates a bar/bat mizvah, the parents are publicly affirming their decision to raise him Jewishly. You will need to check with your rabbi for guidance on the non-Jewish parent's role in the *tallit* presentation or *bimah* honors. When one parent is a Jew by choice, of course there is full participation. In addition, the converted parent may feel that the child's coming of age reconfirms his or her earlier decision. Ideally, the non-Jewish grandparents, aunts, uncles and cousins will be supportive or at least neutral about the upcoming bar/bat mitzvah ceremony, though this may not always be the case. At this life cycle passage, feelings may become sharpened calling for extra sensitivity.

Where there is separation, divorce or remarriage, put the interests of the child ahead of your feelings. However difficult the situation may be, put your issues aside and focus on the best interests of your child. In the long-term, the entire family will benefit from these compromises.

There are no simple answers. When sharing honors, make time to listen to family members' expectations and to respond to them accordingly. Ultimately, decisions must be made based on your individual family dynamics and the guidance of your congregational leaders. A lot of emotion flows upon this occasion.

Hagbah and Glilah

After the reading is completed, the Torah is returned to the *Aron ha-Kodesh* (Holy Ark). Before this takes place, two persons are given the honor of lifting and dressing the Torah, the *hagbah* and *glilah*, respectively. They are usually called up at the same time. Both of these are significant honors, although neither involves saying blessings aloud.

There is a special technique for lifting and displaying the Torah to the congregation. It involves sliding the Torah partially off the reading table and bending your knees to lever it up while you straighten up. This takes some strength, so do not call on an aged relative for this honor. The scroll is heavy and can be quite unbalanced at the beginning or end of the annual cycle, when most of the parchment rests on one handle. We don't wish to make it sound more complicated than it is, but it may be wise to have someone who has done this before serve as *hagbah*. Rolling and dressing takes place after the Torah has been held aloft. The *gabbai*, who helps direct the Torah service from the reading table, will assist the *glilah* in doing this according to custom. The Torah must be tied with a sash and the mantle or cover replaced. If there is a silver breastplate, that goes on after the cover. The yad and crown or finials, if there are any, go on last. If acceptable to your congregation, it might be nice to offer this honor to a grandmother or other woman you wish to have participate in the service.

To assist you in keeping track of the honors you distribute, there is an Aliyot and Honors Chart in the Chart and Timetable Section at the end of this book.

Possibilities for lay participation will differ in each congregation. Consult your rabbi or ritual committee to explore these options. Some synagogues have a Torah reader; others may have a Torah reading club which prepares members of the congregation to read each week, and there are other variations. At one Bat Mitzvah, four women, friends of the family, chanted from the Torah before the Bat Mitzvah was called up. They affectionately became known as the "four matriarchs of Israel." In this way, through personal example, the meaning of the service was enriched for the Bat Mitzvah and her family.

Perhaps a friend or relative could deliver a few remarks from the pulpit in honor of the occasion. This could take the form of a *d'var Torah* or a personal speech about the meaning of this special moment. The speaker must choose his words carefully to fit within the format of this religious service. Sometimes, as a father presents the tallit to his son, he takes this opportunity to say a few words to his son, noting how proud he is as his son acknowledges his religious responsibility to the Jewish community. But any speaker should avoid speaking in an overly sentimental way about childhood episodes and other anecdotes which may embarrass your teenager in this public setting.

Sharing the Spotlight with Siblings

A Bar/Bat Mitzvah is very important for the child and his immediate family. Focusing the spotlight so clearly on one child sometimes brings out unexpected behavior on the part of the siblings, especially if they are younger and have not had this experience themselves. We have seen a slightly younger sister, obviously seeking attention, spend the entire morning running up and down the aisles of the sanctuary. One younger brother stepped out for a drink and never returned. When the rabbi spoke with pride about that youngster's forthcoming Bar Mitzvah, the child was nowhere to be seen. Another little sister stationed herself in the parking lot, grabbing the attention of those arriving for the Bat Mitzvah service. This type of behavior can be avoided by giving siblings a part in the service and understanding their feelings.

Brothers and sisters should be given a role in the Bar/Bat Mitzvah, if possible. Their participation will help them appreciate the meaning of this important Jewish ritual. Naturally, parents must consider the strengths and interests of each child. A clearly more competent older sibling or a cute younger one should not be allowed to overshadow the Bar/Bat Mitzvah child. At one Bar Mitzvah, a much younger, pigtailed little sister led the closing prayer and quite visibly won the hearts of all the congregation. While brothers and sisters should have a share in the Bar/Bat Mitzvah service, planning for their participation takes thought and sensitivity. These plans should be discussed with the Bar/Bat Mitzvah child so he understands how and why his siblings will be involved.

Brothers and sisters should know that they are expected to remain at the ceremony. This special day deserves their cooperation. In many cases, a sibling had or will have this important opportunity himself, and now is the moment to give the Bar/Bat Mitzvah the center of the stage. If a sibling is very young, a relative or good friend should look after the child during the service, leaving the parents free to give their attention to the Bar/Bat Mitzvah. Your child has prepared long and hard for this ceremony and should not have to deal with distractions from his siblings.

How can brothers and sisters become involved in the Bar/Bat Mitzvah ceremony in a meaningful way? There are a variety of possibilities, depending on your children and the nature of your child's Bar/Bat Mitzvah service. An older sibling can be called up for an *aliyah* or to read a Torah portion. A younger sibling may lead a song or prayer. We have seen youngsters wait patiently and then lead the *motzi* right before the food is served. Some congregations have a custom of throwing candy at the Bar/Bat Mitzvah child on the *bimah* when he has completed his *Haftarah* readings. This is a sign of rejoicing as the child has fulfilled his promise. A younger member of the family may be given the responsibility of distributing wrapped candies to those in the congregation, beforehand, so this can take place. Whatever you decide upon, this special participation will be important and help the sibling identify positively with his brother or sister's Bar/Bat Mitzvah experience.

If you want to involve brothers or sisters, or other family members or friends, the Bar/Bat Mitzvah service can offer an opportunity for them to participate. It all depends on the customs of your synagogue and the synagogue skills of your relatives and friends. Be certain to review these options carefully and to give accurate instructions to those sharing the honors. By maximizing your guests' involvement, you will add to the meaning of the Bar/Bat Mitzvah ceremony, setting a fine example for all who are there.

NOTES:

Providing
the Traditional
Ritual Items

Providing the Traditional Ritual Items

While preparing for your child's Bar/Bat Mitzvah, you should be aware of the ritual objects which may be needed for this occasion and for future use. Behind each Jewish symbol lies a long history and tradition. Knowing the background of each of these objects will help you select the ritual items needed.

Head Coverings

Covering one's head is a traditional Jewish sign of respect for God; however, the hat itself has no inherent sanctity. The Torah prescribed that priests cover their heads when engaged in Temple service. And the sages have proclaimed, "Cover your head so that reverence for God be upon you."[1] Covering one's head symbolizes that there is something higher than man. From these roots developed the custom of wearing a head covering, especially when entering a house of study or worship.

Does your congregation expect men and/or women to wear head coverings in the sanctuary? If so, any hat will suffice but typically a man uses a specific lightweight head covering, known by various names: *kipah* (Hebrew), *kipot* (plural), *yarmulke* (Yiddish), and skullcap (English). If customarily worn at your synagogue, standard black *kipot* are usually available in a bin outside the sanctuary. It is possible to order matching ones to give out on the Bar/Bat Mitzvah day. These caps come in many shapes, fabrics, and designs. If you anticipate more than one Bar/Bat Mitzvah in your family, you might consider imprinting them inside with the family name, for example, "Feldman Bar Mitzvah," so you can use them again for your next child. Some families only provide matching *kipot* for the men in the immediate family: Bar Mitzvah boy, brothers, father, uncles, grandfathers. This way, they stand out as a recognizable group. You may purchase these caps or perhaps you have a talented friend or relative who would enjoy crocheting or embroidering a set for you. *The Jewish Catalog,* Volume I, pages 49–50, give detailed instructions and patterns for

---

1. Rabbi Hayim Halevy Donin, *To Pray as a Jew* (New York: Basic Books, Inc., 1980).

making *kipot*. Remember that providing special *kipot* for your congregation is an optional expense which you do not have to incur. Though one *kipah* may be inexpensive, a large number can be costly. Keep in mind that head coverings should not be treated as if they were party favors.

Whether women are expected to wear hats may not be as clearly defined. If married women cover their heads in your synagogue, you should suggest that your female guests wear hats as part of their regular outfit that day. Otherwise, little lace veils with hair pins are often provided for this purpose in a bin outside the sanctuary. If you feel that more of them may be needed, they can be ordered in quantity through a Judaica shop or a catalogue.

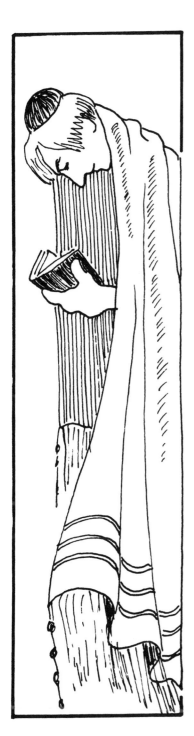

Tallit: A Prayer Shawl with Tzitzit

A *tallit* is customarily worn in many synagogues. In many congregations today, women as well as men wear prayer shawls. A *tallit* is a composite garment made up of a shawl with the essential *tzitzit* or fringes attached to its corners. The word *tallit* comes from the Aramaic, meaning "to cover." The tradition of wearing a *tallit* is based on God's command found in Numbers 15:37–40:

> And the Lord spoke unto Moses, saying: "Speak unto the children of Israel and bid them that they make them throughout their generations fringes in the corners of their garments, and that they put with the fringe of each corner a thread of blue. And it shall be unto you for a fringe, that ye may look upon it, and remember all the commandments of the Lord, and do them; and that ye go not about after your own heart and your own eyes, after which ye used to go astray; that ye may remember and do all My commandments, and be holy unto your God."

Thus, the fringes serve as a tangible reminder of God's commandments to the Jewish people.

In ancient days, Jews wore a free-flowing cloak with fringes attached to the corners. In this way, *tzitzit* were part of their everyday clothing. As time passed and clothing became more elaborate, people no longer attached fringes directly to their outer garments. New garments evolved to allow the observant Jew to fulfill the mitzvah of wearing *tzitzit*. A *tallit katan*, with its fringes, is still worn by many Orthodox Jews every day as an undergarment. Another development was to reserve the *tallit* as a ritual item for use at times of prayer. The sage Maimonides emphasized that the *tallit* should be worn especially when praying; thus, the prayer shawl became an important ritual object that is used in many synagogues to this day.

The *tallit* reflects many levels of religious symbolism. Since Hebrew letters also stand for numbers, Jewish mystics used numerology to emphasize the significance of *tzitzit*. They calculated that the numerical value of the word *tzitzit* = 600. To this, they add the 5 knots and the 8 threads used in fashioning the fringes, which adds up to 613. This is equivalent to the total number of commandments given by God to the Jewish people in the Torah. They maintain that the wearing of the *tzitzit* is therefore a visible reminder to observe all of God's commandments.

If prayer shawls are usually worn in your congregation, the synagogue typically will provide extras on racks outside the sanctuary for those coming without their own. Ushers can direct people to take a *tallit* before entering the service.

Selecting a Tallit

Selecting a *tallit* is a preliminary step in preparing for the Bar/Bat Mitzvah ceremony. One may be found in a Jewish religious shop or in a synagogue gift shop. Or one can buy a *tallit* in Israel or have one made by a knowledgeable Jewish craftsperson. Whatever your choice, make certain that your child likes it and can wear it comfortably without it slipping and sliding off of his shoulders. You can buy very attractive *tallit* clips to alleviate this problem.

The exact construction of a *tallit* follows a prescribed pattern based on specifications set down in the Torah (refer to Numbers 15:37–40). Specific instructions for making a prayer shawl and knotting the fringes can be found in the *Jewish Catalog,* Vol. 1, pages 52–57.

The collar on the *tallit* is called an *atara*. While the *atara* itself has no religious significance, it is used to mark one side of the *tallit* so that the *tallit* is always put on in the same manner. Without the *atara* it would be impossible to know the top from the bottom. A *tallit* will come with its own *atara,* or if you wish to make your own, you can do so. We have seen beautiful *atarot* which have been done in needlepoint or cross-stitch. This is a nice touch which can be used to personalize the *tallit*.

Often the parent presents the child with a *tallit* during the service. He may use this occasion to say a prayer and a few words of praise to his child. Before wrapping himself in the prayer shawl and ascending to the Torah, the Bar/Bat Mitzvah child usually says the blessing for the *tallit:*

> Blessed are You, Lord our God, Ruler of the universe, who hast sanctified us with His commandments and commanded us to wrap ourselves in *tzitzit*.

Customs differ about when one may start to wear a *tallit*. In some congregations the child is presented with a prayer shawl during the bar/bat mitzvah ceremony as a tangible symbol of his coming of age. In other synagogues, the child may wear the *tallit* only at his bar mitzvah and not again until he is married. This tradition is based on the fact that the commandment concerning *tzitzit* is followed by a reference to taking a wife (Deut. 22:12–13).

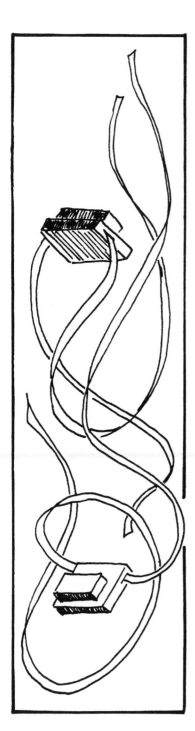

Tefillin

If your child will be wearing a prayer shawl, he may also wear *tefillin* at weekday morning prayers after his Bar Mitzvah. As a Bar Mitzvah, it is both a privilege and an obligation to perform certain religious rites, and the use of *tefillin* is usually included as part of Bar Mitzvah instruction. Though traditionally Jewish women did not wear *tefillin*, today a few young women are choosing to do so. They point to rabbinic legend which speaks of several prominent Jewish women who took part in this ritual.

Tefillin give a Bar Mitzvah something sacred and specific as a sign of his coming of age in the Jewish community. *Tefillin* are a symbolic reminder of man's relationship with God and their use is part of the totality of Jewish religious expression. Whether or not you put on *tefillin*, it is important to support this and other parts of your child's Jewish education. At this point in the history of American Jewry, many children are more interested than their parents were in the symbols of their heritage. Ethnic identity is seen in a positive light. One rabbi we know believes that it is extremely important to perpetuate our distinct religious symbolism so that our children will know the "mystery and magic" of our own faith. Cults and other mind-controlling groups may then have less appeal, for these Jewish youngsters will have a rich ritual heritage of their own with which to identify.

What are Tefillin?

Tefillin are two cubical leather containers with leather straps attached. One is the *tefillin shel yad* for the arm and hand and the other is the *tefillin shel rosh* for the head. Inside each is a piece of parchment upon which a scribe has written four prescribed biblical passages referring to God's kingship, the unity of God, the deliverance of the Jewish people from Egyptian bondage, and the law commanding the use of *tefillin*.

Why Are Tefillin Used as Part of Jewish Ritual?

The use of *tefillin* is commanded four times in the Torah. One time is in the *Sh'ma,* which holds a central place in all of Jewish prayer, which states (Deut. 6:4–8):

Hear, O Israel: The Lord our God, the
Lord is one.
And thou shalt love the Lord, thy God
with all thy heart, and with all thy
soul, and with all thy might.
And these words, which I command thee
this day, shall be upon thy heart;
and thou shalt teach them diligently
unto thy children, and shalt talk of
them when thou sittest in thy house,
and when thou walkest by the way, and
when thou liest down, and when thou risest up.
And thou shalt bind them for a sign upon
thy hand, and they shall be for frontlets
between thine eyes.

Putting on *tefillin* interrupts the continuous demands of everyday life by focusing one's attention on God. In fact, the word *tefillin* comes from the same root as the Hebrew word for prayer, *tefillah,* and these two words are closely connected in meaning. Binding one's arm and head is meant not only as a physical act but also as a spiritual experience. The *tefillin* serve as a symbolic reminder of the entire Torah. Recalling the exodus from Egypt, we are reminded that God freed the Jewish people from physical slavery in Egypt so that they could be bound to the service of God instead.

Why Are Tefillin Connected to the Ritual of Bar Mitzvah?

The use of *tefillin* begins at the age of religious responsibility, the time of Bar Mitzvah. Boys typically are taught the prayers and customs pertaining to *tefillin* as part of their preparation for Bar Mitzvah. Traditional practices vary and therefore, it is a good idea to learn the use of *tefillin* from a teacher belonging to your own congregation. If you need further assistance, you can turn to *The Jewish Catalog,* Vol. I, pages 58–63, Rabbi Hayim Halevy Donin's *To Pray as a Jew,* pages 33–37, or Martin Sandberg's book, *Tefillin: and you shall bind them . . .* for detailed diagrams, descriptions, and the accompanying prayers. Participating in the ritual of *tefillin* is the most visible sign of coming of age. Beginning this religious obligation was an important part of the Bar Mitzvah ceremony. Traditionally, in Eastern Europe, the

Bar Mitzvah was held on a Monday or Thursday with the first use of *tefillin* a public ritual marking that day. Recently, we attended a Bar Mitzvah on a Labor Day Monday, where grandfather, father, and son all laid *tefillin* together. It was very moving to see this commandment being observed by three generations simultaneously, reflecting the passing on of Jewish ritual from generation to generation.

Tefillin are not used on Shabbat. The reason for this is that Shabbat itself is a reminder of God and his creation; therefore, *tefillin*, as a sign, become superfluous. Because the majority of Bar Mitzvah ceremonies now take place at Saturday services, the use of *tefillin* is no longer an integral part of the Bar Mitzvah ceremony. But, having reached the age of religious responsibility, a thirteen-year-old can participate in the ritual of *tefillin* starting the day after his Bar Mitzvah service.

How Do You Buy Tefillin?

Selecting *tefillin* should be done with great care. *Tefillin* must be made to certain specifications and must be hand-written on a piece of parchment made from a kosher animal. The parchment is treated with lime to lighten the color. The *sofer* must make his own quill pen from a feather and use a particular black ink that is both dark and long lasting. Each word must be copied perfectly without errors. Making *tefillin* is an extremely time-consuming task that few people are qualified to do. Prices vary greatly. *Tefillin* can be found in a Jewish bookstore or religious supply shop, or through a Jewish mail-order catalogue. If you are not personally knowledgeable about *tefillin*, take someone with you who can help or consult your congregational teachers before making your purchase.

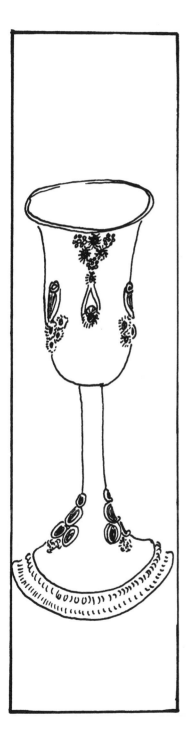

Other Ritual Items: Candlesticks, Kiddush Cup, Challah Cover

Other Jewish ritual items are used at the time of Bar/Bat Mitzvah. Shabbat candlesticks, a *kiddush* cup, and a *challah* cover will probably be needed either at the synagogue or at your own home. The Friday evening synagogue service typically includes the blessings for Shabbat candles, wine, and *challah*. On Saturday morning, the *kiddush* for wine and the *motzi* for *challah* are said before drink and food are tasted. Your congregation will undoubtedly provide the ritual objects for these blessings. However, you may want to use your own personal ones. In one family, a talented relative embroidered a magnificent *challah* cover as a gift for the Bat Mitzvah. She was delighted and honored to see it used as part of the actual Bat Mitzvah ceremony.

If you will be serving Friday night dinner or Saturday lunch at home, you will want to maintain the religious nature of this occasion. To participate in the traditional Jewish rituals, you may want to use Shabbat candlesticks, a *kiddush* cup, and a *challah* cover. Your celebration at home should convey to your guests that this is not just a Friday night dinner party or Saturday luncheon, but rather a meal shared by family and friends to rejoice at a religious passage. Participating in the traditional Jewish rituals will set this celebration apart from an ordinary social event and convey the appropriate tone for this special occasion.

NOTES:

The Invitation

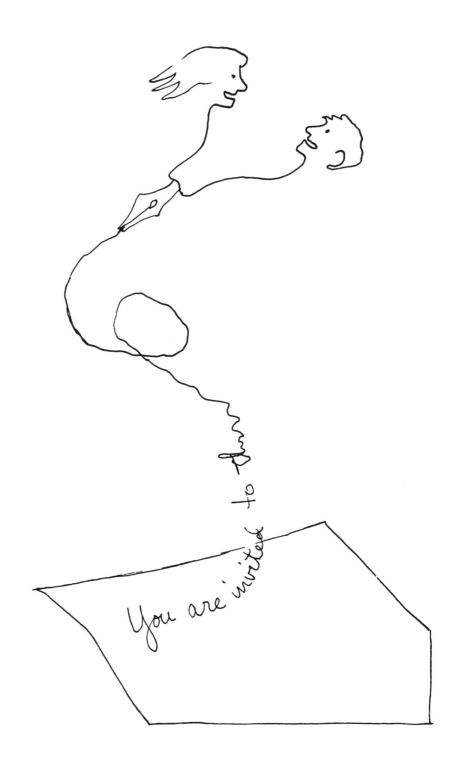

You are invited to dinner

The Invitation

About six months prior to your child's Bar/Bat Mitzvah date, you should begin selecting or designing the invitation. Allow sufficient time, whether you choose and order them from a commercial printer's samples, or design and print them on your own. Decide beforehand what you want to convey, for the invitation can help set the tone for the occasion. With a little planning, the entire process need not be complicated.

One good idea is to save Bar/Bat Mitzvah invitations you've received over the years. They may serve as models when you plan your own child's invitation. Friends may help you by sharing details on where they obtained their invitations.

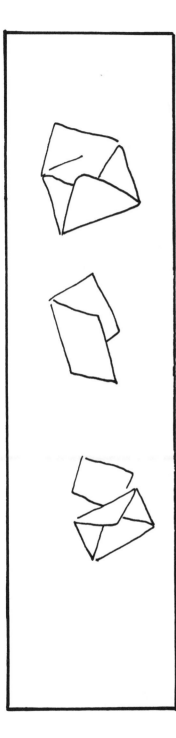

Standard Printed Invitations

Using standard printed invitations is an easy way to handle this part of your preparations. These invitations vary widely in style, message, and cost. After some comparison shopping, you should be able to find one which expresses your personal message well while fitting your budget. Depending on where you live, you probably can order this type of invitation from your Jewish bookstore or synagogue shop. They also may be found in display binders containing sample invitations of different types at a gift shop or the stationery section of a department store. Before you order, study the available samples to refine your ideas for wording and format, then specify how your individual selection should appear. Make certain that you allow enough time for the order to be handled, even with some unexpected delay. When placing the final order, find out if it's possible to take the envelopes home before the invitations are printed. This will allow you extra time to begin addressing the envelopes.

Designing Your Own Invitation

If you prefer, you can design your own invitation. It can take one of many forms depending on your personal talents, the assistance you can get from friends and professionals, and how simple or complex you want the end product to be. With the following guidelines, you should be able to design and duplicate your own composition. The entire invitation can be printed on the front side of a sturdy card. If you wish a more elaborate format, you may want to work with a folded note. The printing can still be done in one operation, but folding the paper will allow you to have a design on the front as well as a message inside. The front may carry a quotation from the Torah or

Haftarah portion for the Bar/Bat Mitzvah or a quote from the rabbis or Jewish wisdom literature. This may be written in Hebrew with the translation or in English, depending on your taste. An original design on the front, whether done professionally or by the parent or child, may also be inspired by the Torah/Haftarah readings for that week. If the ceremony falls during a holiday season, your graphic might reflect, for example, the harvest of *Sukkot* or the candles of *Chanukah*. Here are a few examples of original Bar/Bat Mitzvah invitations to give you an idea.

Because of joy, the heart opens.
Rabbi Nachman of Brazlav

מתנאל

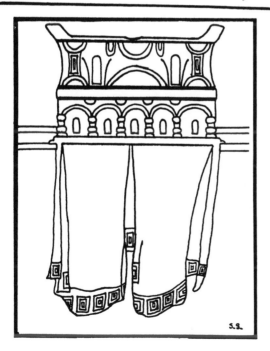

In any case, such a sketch or quotation will add a distinctively Jewish tone to the invitation. Inside one originally designed invitation, it read, "As my father and grandfathers before me, it is now I who will be privileged as a Bar Mitzvah to stand at the pulpit and chant my Haftarah . . ." Whatever your selection, you can communicate to those invited that your Bar/Bat Mitzvah is much more than an occasion for a party: it is a special Jewish religious ceremony.

When designing your own invitation, there are many factors to consider when dealing with printers. There are many different processes which can be used to reproduce invitations: Xeroxing, instant print, standard printing techniques, engraving, and silk screening. With new photographic and computer developments, these processes are continually changing and improving. In deciding how to do your invitations, you will have to evaluate the expense, the time involved in developing a finished product, and the technical expertise needed to prepare the original for duplication. Speak with a printer to examine the various options so that you understand exactly what is involved. Some printers can be extremely helpful in outlining what needs to be done and by giving you instructions on how to do it. Find someone who is willing to answer your questions. Since some techniques are simple, quick, and inexpensive, it is possible for a person without printing experience to prepare and duplicate his own original Bar/Bat Mitzvah invitations. Note also that the printing business is competitive and prices can vary widely within the same city. Therefore, it is best to ask for personal recommendations and to get more than one proposal.

Whatever process you use, consider some or all of the following: type style, paper weight, ink colors, envelope size to match the invitation, and how the design and writing will look when reproduced. You must work within the technical guidelines specified by the individual printer. We know someone who did a detailed drawing in blue ink and then found out that it could only be duplicated from a black ink original. Preparing an oversized original or master artwork may be desirable if the printer is able to reduce it for the copies. Using a broad, felt-tip pen on a large sheet of poster board will allow you to make an original large enough for reduction, a process which makes for a finer finished product. Instead of plain lettering, you may prefer to use calligraphy. If you are not able to do this yourself, check the bulletin board at your Jewish community center or Jewish bookstore and the classified section of your local Jewish newspaper. You're very likely to find a calligrapher looking for work. We stress these sources for you may want someone who can hand letter in Hebrew as well as English.

A creative and less expensive method is to generate invitations via computer. If you own or have access to a desk-top publishing program, you may be able to do the whole process yourself. If your child is interested in sketching and/or computers, he can take pride in designing his own invitation. With English and Hebrew fonts and Jewish clip art on programs such as Print Shop, you can create an original design. The outcome whether in black and white or in color can be very attractive. Two companies providing computer software for this purpose are: Davka/ (800) 621-8227 or FAX (312) 262-9298 and Kabbalah Software/ (908) 572-0891 or FAX (908) 572-0869.

Another inexpensive way to make an invitation is to purchase notecards with an attractive design. You can write or type your message on the card. Then take the sample to a printer who will print the same message on each card. Before purchasing the cards, consult a printer since variances in size may be a consideration for cost, design, and printing.

In the newsletter of some synagogues, it is customary either to announce the forthcoming Bar/Bat Mitzvah or to issue a general invitation to the congregation. Note how this is done at your synagogue so that you can follow the standard procedure.

Remember that 100 or even 50 invitations can be a sizeable expense. However, you need not spend a lot on your invitations in order to have them convey the sentiments you feel.

Parents Who Are Separated or Divorced

If the parents are separated or divorced, the basic invitation can be worded the same as that of a child whose parents are married. The only difference is that the parents may want to list their names on two different lines at the bottom of the invitation. Or, if you wish to acknowledge the step-parents, their names can be included as well. For example:

Barbara and David Goldberg
and
Joseph and Cheryl Stein

In this way, you may avoid hurt feelings. It's a good idea to enclose return cards and envelopes for RSVP's since some guests may only know one parent. These return envelopes can be addressed directly to the Bar/Bat Mitzvah child, thereby avoiding the use of one parent's name and not the other. In fact, many families find it easier to extend the entire invitation directly from the child.

Additional Inserts and the RSVP

You may be holding a Friday night dinner, a gathering on Saturday night or a family brunch on Sunday. If so, you can simplify your planning by enclosing separate cards for these events along with the original invitation. You may wish to invite a smaller number of guests to your home than to the synagogue service or to invite for Friday night dinner only family and friends from out-of-town. Perhaps your in-laws or a very close friend will be hosting the Shabbat dinner or the Sunday morning brunch. These extra inserts allow you to acknowledge the different hosts or target the out-of-towners for extra hospitality during the weekend. Whatever you choose, decide on the different inserts before placing your final invitation order. Otherwise, you will incur additional costs for the extra printing since there is a set-up fee for each run, no matter how small or large the order.

- Will you be including inserts for hotel accommodations, maps, rental cars, etc. for your out-of-town guests? For more information on this topic, refer to the Guest chapter.

- How will you handle responses? You may enclose a stamped, self-addressed envelope with an RSVP card. This may simplify the process, but will cost extra.
- Another option is to write "RSVP" or "Kindly Respond" on the bottom of the invitation. If you include your telephone number in addition to your return address, be prepared for a series of phone responses.
- Some hosts code the RSVP card on the back with a number in the lower right hand corner. On a master list, each number will correspond to a specific guest. It serves a double purpose. If you have three families named "Cohen" and an RSVP card is returned with "The Cohens will be delighted to join you," you will be sure which Cohens are coming. If someone fails to respond, you can cross-reference the missing number with your master list.

Mailing the Invitations

Out-of-town invitations may be mailed as early as eight weeks before the Bar/Bat Mitzvah to allow guests ample time to make travel arrangements; local invitations should be sent six weeks ahead. This difference in the mailing schedule may give you a little extra time to assist your out-of-town guests with their plans. If some of your relatives live far away and have moved recently, it may take some advance work through the family grapevine to locate their current addresses. Mail all groups of invitations together to avoid possible hurt feelings that may occur if invitations arrive at markedly different times. Include a return address on each envelope so that, if addressed incorrectly, it will be returned to you. At this time, it may be handy to purchase a return-address stamp or embosser which can be used on the invitations and thank-you notes. No matter how carefully you plan, some misunderstandings may occur—an invitation can get lost in the mail or on the recipient's desk. If you do not receive a response in a reasonable time, perhaps the message never arrived. Although you hope for a timely response from your guests, that is not always the case. To follow up on your unanswered invitations, you may find it helpful to have a friend call on your behalf. This avoids embarrassing your guest by having you, the host, place the call. It also allows the calls to be made quickly and simply, freeing you to work on other last minute arrangements.

NOTES:

Guests

The Guest List

Once the date has been selected, you must decide which guests to invite to join you for this joyous occasion. This is a difficult decision and you probably will find that the most difficult part is deciding where to draw the line. As a friend said, "I know that they are wonderful people, but do I have to invite them to the Bat Mitzvah?"

To prepare adequately, you should start thinking about your guest list about six months before the Bar/Bat Mitzvah date. A systematic approach, with certain clear guidelines, can help you make a complete list, avoid overlooking anyone, and simplify your decision making. If you plan ahead thoughtfully, you will remain content with your choices because you'll avoid making impulsive decisions under the strain of last minute pressures.

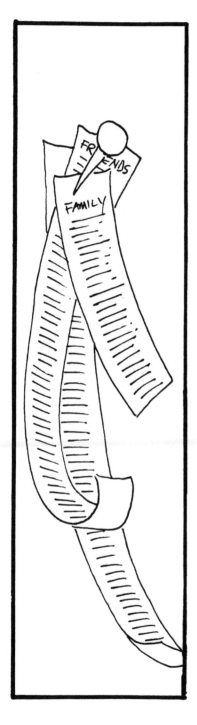

Whom to Invite

As you begin your list, turn to the "Charts and Time-tables" section at the end of this book. These charts will help you organize your list efficiently. Begin by filling in the sheets labeled *Preliminary List* with the following categories:

- Family
- Friends of the parents
- Neighbors
- Child's friends, teachers, and the Bar/Bat Mitzvah tutor
- Professional/business associates
- Members of the congregation, its lay and religious leaders

List names by category to help you recall everyone in the same circle. Ultimately you'll not be able to invite everyone, but now is the time to write the names of all those who should be considered. If you own a computer or have access to one, you should begin entering the names and addresses of all your guests. Having all the information on a computerized list will simplify the process.

You may want to ask the Bar/Bat Mitzvah child if there are any special people he would like to include. List all possible names for inclusion, as if no constraints on numbers existed. Finer distinctions can be made later.

After you've listed all possible guests by category, take a moment to reflect on the group as a whole. A Bar/Bat Mitzvah is a religious ceremony which has meaning for guests of all ages. As an important milestone in your child's life, its significance is enhanced by the presence of young and old alike. Most synagogues welcome children to their services. You may be inviting guests who usually spend Shabbat together as a family, and their interests should be respected. Of course a celebration which includes all members of the guest's family, including children, may be very joyful, but it will be less formal. If you decide to limit your invitations mainly to adults you will have a different type of celebration.

When composing the guest list, avoid the temptation to use the occasion simply to fulfill social obligations. One child said that at her Bat Mitzvah, she did not want to look out upon a sea of unfamiliar faces. Choose guests who know your child and who wish to share this special moment with your family. At another time, you can reciprocate for business and personal obligations.

Completing the Guest List

WITH YOUR PRELIMINARY GUEST LIST DONE, YOU'LL HAVE TO RE-FINE IT AND MAKE YOUR FINAL CHOICES.

First, count the total number of adults and children separately to get an idea of the composition of the group. Second, in the categories of family, friends, and neighbors, see if you've included adults only or all members of each nuclear family. Then, you must decide if you want this day to be mainly for adults or a multigenerational family affair. Whether you include all ages, inviting families not just individuals, is an important decision which will shape the tone of your child's Bar/Bat Mitzvah.

The capacity of your synagogue sanctuary may limit the length of your final guest list. In addition, your budget may put restraints on your expenses. The size of your home and other factors may influence your list as well. You may want to check with your synagogue to see if the Bar/Bat Mitzvah family is expected to sponsor the Friday night *oneg Shabbat* and/or the Saturday morning *kiddush*. Rememer that it is usually possible to modify the festivities to suit the size and scope of your guest list. This is undoubtedly better than restricting your choice of guests because of a fixed reception style. If more people are to be included, you can hold a reception which is less elaborate and less expensive per person. A simple spread will be well received. Good fellowship is far more important than elaborate eating. The primary consideration is to share the joy of the occasion with those who are close to you and your child. Their presence will enhance the meaning of your child's Bar/Bat Mitzvah.

As you see the broad outlines of your guest list taking shape, you will have to begin planning the festivities. Sufficient lead time is needed for making those arrangements, so don't put off the final difficult decisions. Begin developing general plans for a celebration to accommodate your guests. The chapter "Extending the Festivities with a Party" gives useful guidance in this area.

After a few weeks you should review each preliminary guest category to see if any names should be omitted or relegated to "optional" status. Some previously overlooked names may come to mind after that bit of time has elapsed. Have you invited all those relatives who are related to you in the same way? Did you include all your first cousins and their children or just the ones with whom you are close? Will the ones you left out be angry with you for years to come?

In a few weeks you'll be reviewing the lists for the third and final time. Make decisions on those marked "optional," realizing that a line must be drawn somewhere. Everyone in your club, school, or social circle cannot be there or your celebration will lose form entirely. These are hard limits to set, ones which the Bar/Bat Mitzvah parents must do with thought and care. You should reassure yourself that not everyone you know can be invited.

Without a doubt, uninvited friends and neighbors will be talking to you about the Bar/Bat Mitzvah. Inevitably, someone you did not invite will bump into you in the hardware store. This is not the time to tell her that you somehow accidentally overlooked her name and would she and her husband please come to this Saturday's service. Your tennis partner may ask how everything is going. If she does not know your child, you must remember that there is a great gap between the tennis court and the *bimah*. Only a limited number of people can be invited and that decision is under your control. There is no need to be uncomfortable or embarrassed when meeting someone who is not on your list.

Make your final guest list decisions no later than ten weeks before the date, which will give you time to learn to live with your choices. You will inevitably have argued with yourself over those on the questionable list right up to this deadline. At this final moment, it is better to err on the side of including extras rather than drawing the line too tight. At this point, if one parent still feels that a certain person should be included, he should be invited. There always seems to be enough room and food for a few more. If your reception does not involve being seated with placecards, a few extra will not matter. If you complete your choices ten weeks beforehand, you will have no regrets for there is enough time to handle any changes before any of the invitations are mailed.

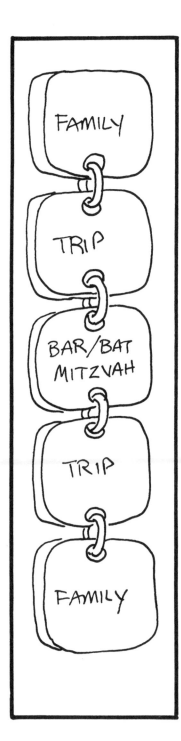

Out-of-Towners

It is true that a Bar/Bat Mitzvah often becomes the setting for a family to convene from far and wide. In past generations, the extended family—aunts, uncles, sisters, brothers, and cousins—often lived within a few miles of each other and may even have belonged to the same congregation. Today, with children leaving home for college or job transfers, and with grandparents often retiring to the Sun Belt, many families are scattered all over the country.

Since out-of-town guests must travel to the Bar/Bat Mitzvah, they'll benefit from your anticipation of their specific needs. It is this group of guests which adds an entire new dimension to your planning. They have come to town specifically to be with you on this important occasion. At Bar/Bat Mitzvah ceremonies we have attended, the rabbi often extends a personal word of welcome to guests who've come from afar. He mentions their respective homes because the distance they've traveled reflects the importance of this occasion.

Lodging: Home Hospitality or Hotel Reservations

WHAT CAN BE DONE TO MAKE OUT-OF-TOWNERS FEEL WELCOME AND COMFORTABLE FOR THE DURATION OF THEIR VISIT?
You can help by providing convenient and suitable accommodations. The Bar/Bat Mitzvah weekend will be very busy for your immediate family and, therefore, not a convenient time for you to have many house guests. Perhaps grandparents, some other relatives, or a close friend could stay with you. The other out-of-towners will also need lodging and meals. Your in-town friends, relatives, and some members of the congregation who live near the synagogue may be eager to share more fully in the joy of this special weekend by offering home hospital-

ity. This can be a positive experience for all, as your local and distant friends and family are afforded the opportunity to get to know each other better. If it's available, be certain to include information about home hospitality along with the basic Bar/Bat Mitzvah invitation.

Perhaps, in your situation, it would be preferable to use a conveniently located hotel or motel. Your out-of-town guests may enjoy staying together for the weekend. If you need a large number of rooms, you should choose these accommodations approximately three months prior to the Bar/Bat Mitzvah. Estimate how many out-of-town guests you expect, and reserve a block of rooms together. Check to see if a discount is offered for this size group, or for senior citizens, which may pertain to some of your guests. Some hotels offer a hospitality suite for the private use of a group booking a large number of rooms. This can be a convenience as a gathering place or as a location for serving family-style meals.

Along with the Bar/Bat Mitzvah invitation sent to out-of-town guests, you may wish to include a brochure from the selected hotel/motel or a Xeroxed sheet describing other possible accommodations. Include specific instructions, telling your guests how they can reserve directly, so that you can stay out of the middle of this time-consuming process. If you choose a national hotel/motel chain, your guests may be assisted by telling them the "800" telephone number to book and confirm reservations. Although you may take the initial step by setting aside a block of rooms, you should expect your out-of-town guests to confirm their reservations and pay for their rooms. However, you may want to provide a warm welcome by leaving a fruit basket, cheese and crackers, or some sweets in each guest's room.

An extremely capable and hospitable Bat Mitzvah mother in Boston did something unusual. She paired each out-of-town family with a local host family. The local host did some or all of the following:

- Met the arriving family at the airport and took them to their motel room.
- Invited them for Friday night dinner.
- Transported the out-of-towners to the Bat Mitzvah events so that they would not have to rent a car.
- Looked after the visiting family during the service and celebration to make certain they were comfortable.
- Returned the traveling family to the airport at the end of the weekend.

Providing for Guests Who Observe Kashrut

Do any of your guests coming from afar observe *kashrut*? How can you help provide for their needs? You may wish to have available paper plates, plastic utensils, and some basic foods marked with the U, Star K or K. If some of your guests keep kosher, while you do not, this may influence the meals you serve over the weekend. Possibly dairy or vegetarian platters would be suitable. If you use host families, pair up your kosher guests with kosher friends if possible. You might check if there are any conveniently located kosher restaurants nearby. Your thoughtfulness will be appreciated.

Friday Night Dinner

Besides the celebration following the Bar/Bat Mitzvah ceremony, will you be serving your out-of-town guests other meals? Do you want to offer Friday night dinner for your arriving guests? This decision may be influenced by whether you plan to attend and participate in the Friday evening services at your synagogue. If you plan to go to services, you may combine this with a dinner at the synagogue. Alternatively, you may simply include a more limited number of guests for a meal at your home.

A friend of ours informally gathered everyone together for a delicatessen platter served in her large kitchen. Upon arrival in town, it was nice to feel immediately welcomed and a part of this special weekend. Otherwise, your local friends or family might be delighted to invite an out-of-town family for Friday night dinner at their home. For any of these plans, you must consider whether your guests will arrive early enough and whether you can handle this extra phase of the weekend. If you can arrange it, Friday night dinner can be a lovely opening celebration.

Sunday Brunch

A Sunday brunch at your home is another hospitable touch. This more intimate gathering is a nice way to continue your celebration throughout the weekend. It may include those coming from afar, as well as your local family and special friends. A brunch can be simple and quite informal, with self-service and paper plates. It can consist of some of the leftovers from your Saturday party, along with food that you have prepared in advance and frozen. A basic cold brunch buffet may be ordered from a local delicatessen, caterer, or the supermarket. Or you may want to do something a little unusual. This may be a good time to hire a local firm which comes to the house to cook omelets or crepes. Another suggestion for the Sunday morning breakfast comes from Sephardic friends. At a special breakfast on Sunday, traditionally the father presents his son with a pair of *tefillin*. The father then takes the opportunity to teach his child how to put on *tefillin* in the proper manner. Any of these possible brunch plans should work well. Carefully evaluate how much you can do ahead, how much

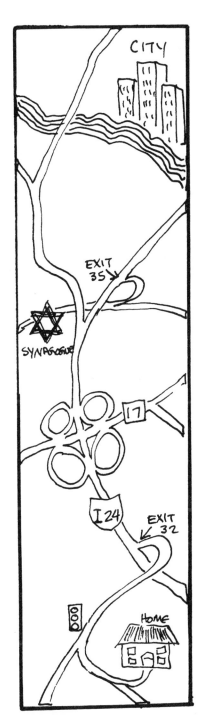

you can do when the time comes, how much you can spend, and then make your decision.

Maps, Directions, and Schedules for the Weekend

Be sure to send local maps and clear directions to all guests who need them. There is no need for them to study gas station maps or ask directions of pedestrians, when you can plan ahead and avoid that problem altogether. Make sure your directions are clear and correct. At a suburban New Jersey Bar Mitzvah, one turn was mistakenly omitted from the directions and two carloads of out-of-town cousins became hopelessly lost on a street with the right name but in the wrong place. Their unexpected delay severely disrupted the service while people already there nervously looked for them. This confusion was totally unnecessary.

As the host, you should write simple but accurate directions covering three locations: the synagogue, the guest's lodging, and your home. Photocopy a section of the local map that includes these three places and, in three distinct colors, mark routes from lodging to synagogue, synagogue to home, and home to lodging. Add directions to the reception if that is held in a different place. You may also want to prepare directions for those coming into town by car or from the airport. Even a taxi driver may need to be directed to your specific area, and guests feel more comfortable when they have a general idea of the route they are to follow.

The care and thought that you put into the directions will assist everyone. Keep copies of all these instructions for some guest inevitably will misplace his and contact you for duplicates at the last moment. You can also save them for use at your next Bar/Bat Mitzvah.

You may include the extras such as maps, directions and schedules as additional inserts when you originally mail your invitation. Having one complete mailing saves you time and the trouble and expense of additional mailings. More importantly, it might encourage some families to make an effort to come when they see how much is planned for the weekend. Otherwise, you may wish to wait for guests to respond that they are coming before sending the extra information. Whatever you choose, make sure your directions and maps are clear and correct.

Our Boston friend, who arranged for host families, left an information packet at each guest's place of lodging. In this packet the Bat Mitzvah family extended a personal welcome and described the schedule of services and festivities for the weekend. The packet may also include data or newspaper clippings about nearby places of interest, possible walking tours, and local events. We know a Bar Mitzvah family with a large number of children, who wrote brief articles about their family, published it via computer, photocopied the resulting newspaper and distributed it with the welcoming package. The out-of-town friends and relatives had a chance to read about the Bar Mitzvah boy and his siblings. The relatives commented that the newspaper made them more aware of the children's interests and gave them topics to discuss with the kids. It was a nice touch that cost very little money and made the guests feel welcomed.

If there is some leisure time, your guests might enjoy exploring the unique sights of your community. One family, who lived just outside Washington, D.C., arranged for a chartered bus and guide to take the out-of-towners on an historical tour in lieu of a Saturday night party. In Kansas City, another family hired an antique trolley for a Sunday morning tour before brunch.

Whatever effort you make on behalf of your guests, all of them, especially the elderly and those with small children, will appreciate it. The fewer arrangements they have to make for themselves, the easier and more enjoyable their trip to the Bar/Bat Mizvah will be.

אֵשֶׁת חַיִל מִי יִמְצָא,
וְרָחֹק מִפְּנִינִים מִכְרָהּ
בָּה לֵב בַּעְלָהּ, וְשָׁלָל
לֹא יֶחְסָר:

מִי חַיֶּיהָ, כָּל
בְּחֵפֶץ

UNDERSTANDING
THE SERVICE

טוֹב וְלֹא־רָע, כָּל
צֶמֶר וּפִשְׁתִּים, וַתַּעַשׂ
כָּאֳנִיּוֹת סוֹחֵר, מִמֶּרְחָק
בְּעוֹד לַיְלָה, וַתִּתֵּן טֶרֶף
שָׂדֶה וַתִּקָּחֵהוּ, מִפְּרִי

Explaining the Service

Some of your guests may be unfamiliar with the religious service and customs at your synagogue. Although the prayer book is a guide, you may find it useful to write a brief overview of the service and the Bar/Bat Mitzvah's role in it. This can be mailed ahead of time or placed at the entry to the synagogue on the Bar/Bat Mitzvah day.

Here is a sample letter from one Bat Mitzvah family:

Shabbat Shalom and Welcome

On this Sabbath, we will be celebrating Rachel's becoming a Bat Mitzvah. We hope these notes will make the ceremony more meaningful for you.

Rachel's participation as a Bat Mitzvah is incorporated into the weekly service. At your seat is a Torah in book form and a Shabbat prayer book. These books are written in both Hebrew and English. During the service, the rabbi will indicate when prayers should be said standing or sitting, aloud or silently. The cantor will chant the prayers and will lead us in responses.

The Sabbath morning service is divided into several distinct parts.

PRELIMINARY SERVICE—Prayers in this section prepare the worshipper for the morning service. These selections praise and acknowledge God. Readings are drawn largely from the Psalms.

SHACHARIT—This begins with a formal call to prayer. It centers on the *Shema*, the cardinal principle of Judaism, "Hear, O Israel, the Lord our God, the Lord in One." It also includes the *amidah* which is said individually as one stands.

TORAH SERVICE—The Torah is a scroll, handwritten on parchment by a scribe. It contains the Five Books of Moses. The Torah is the holiest object of the Jewish people. When the Torah is removed from the ark and when it is returned, the congregation rises in respect. The Torah is divided into 54 portions and is read in weekly rotation throughout the year. The portion for this week is *Chayye Sarah* from the book of Genesis. It tells about the life Sarah and Abraham and includes the famous story of Rebecca at the well. As the Torah is read, individuals from the congregation are honored with an aliyah, to say the blessings before and after each Torah portion. To prepare for her Bat Mitzvah, Rachel has been studying the Torah and the *Haftarah* with their distinctive melodies. When the Torah portion is completed, the *Haftarah*, a related reading from the Prophets, is chanted. When Rachel finishes chanting, she will give a brief talk, *d'var Torah*, on today's reading.

MUSAF—An additional short service which will conclude with various hymns and a wish for *shabbat shalom*, a peaceful sabbath day.

Then Rachel will recite blessing over the wine and braided challah. We are delighted that you are here with us on this special occasion.

A different approach is a simple sheet which defines the elements of the Bar/Bat Mitzvah.

Vocabulary of the Bar/Bat Mitzvah Service

Here are some words which you may hear during our celebration.

ALIYAH: Literally, going up. Being called up to the Torah to recite a blessing before and after the Torah is read.

AMIDAH: A central prayer said while standing.

BAR OR BAT MITZVAH: Literally, son or daughter of the commandments. A rite of passage, generally at age 13, which signifies entry into religious adulthood.

CANTOR: The person who leads the chanting of the prayer service.

D'VAR TORAH: Literally, words of Torah. A learned speech on some aspect of the weekly Torah portion.

HAFTARAH: The reading from the Prophets following the Torah reading on the Sabbath and festivals.

KIPAH: hat or head covering. Covering one's head follows an ancient Jewish tradition. It is a sign of respect for God, especially in a house of worship. Available in a bin outside the sanctuary.

RABBI: The spiritual leader of the congregation.

SHABBAT SHALOM: Literally, a peaceful sabbath. A customary greeting at the end of services.

SHEMA: The cardinal principle of Judaism, "Hear, O Israel, the Lord our God, the Lord is One."

TALLIT: prayer shawl. Traditionally, Jewish men over 13 wear a tallit at services. In Reform and Conservative congregations, some women also wear a tallit.

TORAH: A scroll, handwritten by a scribe on parchment. It contains the Five Books of Moses and is the holiest object of the Jewish people.

Many friends have begged us to suggest a little warning to some guests. While the invitation may state that 9:15 AM is the starting time, those, who are not at all familiar with practices at your synagogue, often are the first to arrive. You could tell them that meandering in a little later is commonly done. That would make their morning at services a bit shorter and possibly more comfortable.

HOW CAN WE ASSIST PARENTS WHO BRING SMALL CHILDREN TO THE BAR/BAT MITZVAH?

When the whole family is invited, guests may bring infants and toddlers. Providing baby-sitting is a gracious way to welcome families with young children. A word beforehand or a sign at the synagogue will let parents know about the baby-sitting option, and they will appreciate this special assistance.

Many synagogues regularly hire baby-sitters to look after young children during services. If there is a nursery school at the synagogue during the week, these facilities are an ideal location for baby-sitting. Keep in mind that if many young children are invited you may need to engage more than one sitter. In selecting sitters, remember that managing a group of children in a new setting is a big responsibility which demands more competence than taking care of two sleeping children at their own home. You should be certain that toys and books are available. Supply a sufficient amount of juice and cookies for the children since they may be with the sitters for a long time. In some congregations, it is customary for the young children to return to the sanctuary or even to sit on the *bimah* for the concluding songs. By providing a baby-sitter you will be at ease knowing that the service will not be interrupted by restless young guests.

ARE ANY OF YOUR GUESTS SHOMER SHABBAT (STRICT SABBATH OBSERVERS)?

Some of your guests may be *Shomer Shabbat*. To make their visit as comfortable as possible, you should take into consideration where they will be staying, either with a host family or at a hotel. Does the host family keep kosher? If the hosts are not *Shomer Shabbat*, will your guests feel awkward staying with them? Are they within walking distance of your synagogue, or would the walk be a hardship in 85 degree heat or a foot of snow? Might the baby-sitter you've provided ask the children to draw, paste, cut, or watch television? Are you asking these guests to attend a reception outside the synagogue to which they cannot walk? Are you serving only hot, unkosher food which they will not eat? Asking your guests about their particular level of observance will enable you to make them feel at home and avoid embarrassing situations.

ARE THERE CERTAIN PRACTICES AT YOUR SYNAGOGUE WHICH YOUR GUESTS SHOULD KNOW ABOUT?

If you belong to an Orthodox or Conservative congregation, some of the following concerns must be addressed:

> Are married women required to cover their heads?
>
> Is it acceptable for a woman guest to wear a pantsuit?
>
> Would someone using a pay telephone or a soda machine offend members of your congregation?
>
> Would your rabbi or other congregants find it unacceptable to use a camera or tape recorder during the service and reception?
>
> Would someone smoking on the Sabbath cause heads to turn?

We realize that no one seeks to offend, but some people do so out of ignorance. Making your guests aware of the *minhagim* at your synagogue can prevent some awkward and embarrassing situations.

NOTES:

Extending the Festivities With a Party

Extending the Festivities With a Party

The Bar/Bat Mitzvah Party

Hospitality is fundamental to the Jewish way of life. Its importance is emphasized in the first book of the Torah (Genesis 18:1–8) when three strangers arrived at Abraham's tent. His first thought was to offer them refreshment. Five times there are references to how swiftly he carried out this task so that his guests received proper hospitality before continuing on their journey.

A celebration naturally follows the Bar/Bat Mitzvah service. It is appropriate to rejoice with a party afterward. Jewish religious observance typically includes the sharing of food after a *simcha,* whether it be a *brit milah,* a wedding, or a Bar/Bat Mitzvah. The party derives from the custom of serving a *seudah mitzvah* celebrating the performance of a *mitzvah.*

As the Bar Mitzvah ceremony assumed greater importance in fourteenth and fifteenth century Germany and Poland, a festive meal was usually included as part of the celebration. Some traditional sources such as the *Shulhan Arukh* even stated that it was the duty of the father to provide this Bar Mitzvah feast just as he would provide a feast on a wedding day. Therefore, you are helping to preserve an important Jewish custom and fulfilling a *mitzvah,* by giving a party after your child's Bar/Bat Mitzvah ceremony.

The Party Celebrating a Bar or Bat Mitzvah

After your child has been called to join his religious community, there is good reason to rejoice. But in planning, it is important to avoid extremes; good judgment must not be sacrificed. Although a Bar or Bat Mitzvah date is often chosen more than one or two years in advance, it doesn't mean that having all this time should encourage one to have an overly elaborate affair. This is not just a modern concern. For hundreds of years, local Jewish communities were concerned that the feast with its elaborate and possibly wasteful entertainment would detract from the religious significance of the day. Ostentation would undermine the very values which the Bar/Bat Mitzvah seeks to affirm. To avoid this problem, the community developed sumptuary laws to control the style of the celebration. In Poland in 1659, it was decreed that no more than ten strangers might be invited to a Bar Mitzvah feast, among whom there must be one poor man to share in the rejoicing. In Germany, the Jewish communities' regulations to control extravagance were very detailed. In the eighteenth century, the Bar Mitzvah boy was formally forbidden to wear a wig, an aristocratic fashion of the time.[1]

Jews have always celebrated life cycle events. Jewish principles, such as *kashrut* which sanctifies eating and *tzedakah* which reminds us of the justice of sharing our good fortune, give guidance on how to maintain a proper balance. Since today there are no sumptuary laws, you have to rely on your good judgment in shaping the tone of the celebration. You want to keep in mind your goals—celebrating your child's coming of age; surrounding the Bar/Bat Mitzvah with the love of family and friends; conveying Jewish values; serving as a role model for the children; bringing your family together from far and near; plus other personal aims. Strapless dresses for the kids, the money grab game, a Mickey Mouse theme, a flowing hard liquor bar, the mummy wrap do little or nothing to serve your purposes. Nor would following in the wake of *Bernie's Bar Mitzvah*, an off-Broadway production, advertised as "It's a show, it's food, fantasy, it's an audience participation extravaganza. . . ." With less emphasis on the "Bar" and more on the "Mitzvah," you will shape your child's Bar/Bat Mitzvah day into an event that is memorable, warm, and gracious.

1. Abraham Katsh, ed., *Bar Mitzvah, Illustrated* (New York: Shengold Publishers, 1955), pg. 20.

Suggestions For Enhancing Your Party

With Prayers and Blessings

Prayers and blessings are not only said by rabbis and cantors at synagogue services. At your Bar/Bat Mitzvah reception, you can start by saying the *kiddush* over the wine and the *motzi* before eating *challah* or bread. Beginning the meal with these prayers serves to sanctify the day and sets the tone for your celebration.

Deuteronomy 8:10 states "And you shall eat and be satisfied and you shall bless the Lord your God for the goodly land which he gave you." This is the origin of the *Birkat ha-Mazon,* the blessings chanted after a meal. Over the ages, differing versions of the *Birkat* have developed. Your synagogue or a Jewish book store will often have these blessings in booklet form, on laminated cards, or photocopied sheets for you to distribute to your guests. Your guests may easily join in this ritual if the booklets include the Hebrew, a transliteration, and the English translation. Finding a competent leader for the *Birkat* gives you another opportunity to share an honor. Perhaps you can ask someone to lead the blessings who did not receive an *aliyah* at the bar/bat mitzvah service.

With Havdalah

It is a *mitzvah* to recite *Havdalah* after the sun goes down on Saturday evening and it is a beautiful way to begin a Bar/Bat Mitzvah reception. If your party will start at sundown on Saturday or will continue through that time, holding this ceremony will heighten the religious tone of your celebration. Just as lighting the Sabbath candles on Friday evening ushers in Shabbat, so lighting the *Havdalah* candle marks its end. This ceremony, with its prayers, symbols and songs, identifies the Sabbath as a unique day, separate and distinct from the work days of the week. With its blessings for wine, spices and light, *Havdalah* touches all the senses as a new week begins. What do you need to do to make this happen? Look for the service in your prayer book and ask a professional or skilled lay leader to help direct it.

With a Candle-Lighting Ceremony

The candle-lighting ceremony allows you to honor special friends and relatives. This ceremony is a modern innovation which has become very popular. Relatives and friends can be called up with a brief introduction to light a candle and to say a few words about their relationship to the bar/bat mitzvah.

On an easily accessible and easily seen table, place candlesticks with candles already in them. Typically, people use thirteen candles and you can group together friends and relatives if you have more than thirteen to honor. If you cannot make this work, add a few candles but be careful not to make this part of the celebration too long. Have at least one long candle to light all the others. This candle should be dripless and you may even need tinfoil to make sure that no one burns their hands. You, the bar/bat mitzvah child or a sibling can run the event.

Many people compose rhymes about the individuals who they call up to light each candle. These may be written by your child, if he is gifted or interested, or by the family working together. If all else fails, ask a friend who has recently done this. If you have a band or a disc jockey, you can give them a list of music that corresponds to the personality or profession of each person who is called up.

There are many ways that the candle-lighting ceremony can add meaning to your *simcha*:

- On an individual basis, you can honor family members and friends.
- On a larger scale, you can recognize the ties that unite world Jewry by lighting a candle in memory of children who died in the Holocaust or the recent Soviet and Ethiopian emigres to Israel.
- Each candle can represent a different Jewish value such as *tzedakah*, learning, peace, family or community.
- Each person lighting a candle can offer a blessing for the bar/bat mitzvah child.

With Themes having Jewish Content

Themes that relate to Judaism, Jewish heritage and Jewish values can help you organize and enhance your festivities. Invitations, decorations, centerpieces, place cards, table names, even party favors can relate to the chosen theme. Here are some general themes with specific examples which you can easily adapt to your party.

- A JEWISH HOLIDAY near the Bar/Bat Mitzvah date.

At *Sukkot*, overflowing baskets of seasonal fruits can adorn the *bimah* and later the party room. At *Chanukah*, make each centerpiece a *chanukiah* with candles. You can decorate the tables with Hanukah gelt and dreydls. At *Tu b'Shevat*, plant a tree in Israel in honor of each table or each guest. As party favors, give each child a JNF box with a few starter coins towards planting a tree in Israel. At Purim, one friend used styrofoam wig stands as the foundation for dramatic centerpieces. In the spirit of the holiday, she dressed each form with a wig, hat, eyeglasses and jewelry and portrayed different characters of modern times—from Groucho Marx to Golda Meir.

- JEWISH HEROES/HEROINES in historical or modern times

For a hero theme, there are many exciting possibilities. The Bar/Bat Mitzvah child can prepare a speech about his favorite hero or heroine. Such celebrities might include Theodore Herzl, Golda Meir or Moshe Dayan. If you have a David, Deborah,

Jonathan, Joshua, Rachel, Rebecca, your child might want to speak about his or her Biblical namesake. To carry through this theme, favors, table names and decorations can be built around the personality of the hero. Jonah can have whales and a sea theme. Joseph's technicolor dreamcoat theme, inspired by the Andrew Lloyd Webb musical, offers endless starting points for a memorable Bar Mitzvah. Tables could be named for the brothers or for colors and your imagination can take you from there.

• YOUR FAMILY GENEALOGY

One wonderful Bar Mitzvah used family genealogy as its theme. Each table was named for a city where family members came from or presently resided. Roots were traced back to Minsk, Bialystok, and Vienna. Ports of entry were recorded along with the dispersion of the family in the following generations. Speeches by the son and parents elaborated on the unique paths taken by their family members. If you like, you could give a book on genealogy or a blank family tree to each guest. Or perhaps, you would prefer to make a donation to the Holocaust Museum in memory of the children of Europe, who never celebrated a Bar or Bat Mitzvah.

• GEOGRAPHY OF ISRAEL

Israel is a great source of Jewish pride. There are many ways to use Israel inspired themes at your party. The blue and white of the flag can color your invitations, balloons, carnations, tablecloths, and anything else you can think of. Tables can be named for cities such as Tel Aviv, Haifa, Eilat with Jerusalem, the head table. Consult your atlas for more ideas. Use baskets made by Ethiopian Jews and filled with Elite candies as centerpieces. Favors can include "I Love Israel" mugs, tee shirts or key chains.

• JERUSALEM

Jerusalem, the center of the Jewish world, is a wonderful theme for a Bar/Bat Mitzvah party. Name your tables for historic sites such as the Western Wall, Mount of Olives, Ben Yehuda Street, Jaffa Gate, King Solomon's Pool, Hezekiah's Tunnel. If you can, use photographs or write a description of the significance of each historical site. The color scheme can be Israeli blue and white or simply gold since Jerusalem is known as the City of Gold. You can plan a delicious traditional Middle Eastern menu with foods such as humus, pita bread, felafel, babaganoush, and Israeli salad.

• ISRAELI NATURE AND ENVIRONMENT

For the outdoorsy family, the Israel theme can be modified to include various activities one can pursue in Israel. Tables can be named: scuba diving at Eilat; hiking up Masada; skiing on Mt. Hermon; floating in the Dead Sea; swimming in the Mediterranean; boating on the Sea of Galilee; walking in the Old City. You can decorate with posters which may be available through El Al, a Judaic catalogue or your synagogue school. For more information and membership possibilities, contact the Society for the Protection of Nature in Israel at their North American address: 25 West 45th Street, New York, NY 10036, (212) 398-6750. The Nature Company or a Jewish gift catalogue can provide ecology oriented favors. Or perhaps you want to consider a subscription to *Eretz,* the geographic magazine from Israel. Contact them at P.O. Box 1831, Birmingham, AL 35201, (800) 633-4931. Another thought is to plant trees in Israel in honor of your Bar/Bat Mitzvah guests and send each person home with a certificate.

• JEWISH SPORTS FIGURES

A great theme for a bar or bat mitzvah can be developed around Jewish sports heroes. Each table can be dedicated to a different celebrity and his sport, for example Mark Spitz, the Olympic swimmer; Sandy Koufax, the Dodgers pitcher; Shlomo Glickstein, the Israeli tennis star; Barney Ross, the boxer; Irving Jaffee, the Olympic speed skater. Autobiographical material and statistics can be found in books such as Robert Slater's *Great Jews in Sports.* Decorations and favors can relate to the sports theme. On a serious note, the bar/bat mitzvah child could speak of true sports heroes, the Israeli athletes who were massacred at the 1972 Munich Olympics.

Special Ideas for the Kids

Some parents feel that their children want to do something different or are not ready to have a "boy-girl" dance. One suggestion is to hire a competent, older teenager or an adult to organize "ice-breaker" type games. Youth group advisors are usually an excellent source for ideas that work well with young teens. Remember that if you are having a party with both children and adults, everything will run more smoothly if the kids are kept busy with well-organized activities. The best intentioned youngsters may become bored and cause mischief if not properly supervised.

Another suggestion is to plan a party for the teen-agers separate from the bar/bat mitzvah reception. You might talk to other parents in his/her day school or Hebrew school class about arranging a group party. If the class is big, children could co-sponsor a party because their birthdays fall in the same season of the year. Then, the entire class can be invited and this would avoid hurt feelings. Otherwise, parents could organize a party for all the bar and bat mitzvah youngsters at the end of the school year. This would help keep the costs down for such items as a deejay, decorations, and food.

With Personal Touches

- The child can give a *d'var Torah* or bar/bat mitzvah speech. This could include thanks to family, teachers, and others.
- Parents could greet their guests, speak of their feelings on this day, and tell their child how proud they are.
- Personalized booklets can be distributed which include data about the bar/bat mitzvah child and his family. Some old family photos, a family tree, and other information can serve as a take-home memento.
- If your child is surrounded by an enthusiastic group at his table, they could help lead singing at the reception.
- Doing some of the cooking yourself adds a personal flavor to the party. Baking *challah* is an especially nice idea. Recipes can be found in the *Jewish Catalog* and many other Jewish cookbooks.
- Using an alphabet mold, one friend made chocolate lolly-pops with each child's name to use as placecards and party favors.
- One family who live right outside Washington, D.C., arranged for a guided historical tour in lieu of a Saturday night party. In Kansas City, a family hired an antique trolley for a tour before Sunday brunch.
- Another family held a Shabbat morning service and then invited guests back for a Saturday evening sing-along. Their booklet contained thirty-five pages of songs which came from Israel, Yiddish, and modern American pop, folk, and rock singers. Their beautifully illustrated booklet served as a musical party favor.

The Type of Celebration: Number of guests, children, and other variables

In thinking about a party, the first question is where and how to begin planning. Every *seudah mitzvah* will bear the personal imprint of the host family. In developing a helpful timetable, we realize that planning the reception is a three-dimensional puzzle with multiple variables. Different people begin planning their celebration from different starting points. For some, the most important aspect is that all guests be seated; others start by first planning the menu. For some families, the time of sundown and the dietary laws are the critical factors. As with any project, one must decide where to begin developing a solution. One approach is to start by reviewing the size and nature of your guest list; then decide where you will hold the celebration; next plan how food will be served; and finally select the menu. How to serve the meal and what the menu will be should be planned simultaneously, since one has a direct influence on the other.

If your budget will allow it, we feel it best to include all those with whom you wish to share this special occasion, rather than limiting numbers to fit a preconceived party plan. You can reasonably expect that most invited guests will come. Knowing the composition of your group will be a very important factor in determining the type of reception you will have. You should consider how many very young children will be among the guests and how many friends your child wishes to invite. Having counted all these, you will have a clear idea of who will be with you to celebrate.

The time of day the party will be held is another important factor. Are you planning for Friday evening, Saturday afternoon, Saturday evening, or some other time? When is sundown (the beginning or end of Shabbat) that day, and how will that affect your schedule? The season of the year will also influence your decisions. Of course, the foundation of all realistic planning is a budget. Whatever yours is, you can plan for a lovely celebration. This chapter has many suggestions for enhancing your party without great expense.

Facilities Where the Reception May Be Held: Synagogue, home, hotel, or club

Knowing the guest list, time framework, and budget, you can decide where it will be best to hold the reception. Obviously, the synagogue itself is a very suitable place for a Bar/Bat Mitzvah reception. Some synagogues have the facilities necessary for preparing and/or serving food to a large number of guests. This setting is particularly appropriate for it helps maintain the tone of a religious celebration. It simplifies matters because guests won't have to travel elsewhere in a fleet of cars; they simply can walk into your reception area.

The use of a synagogue social hall for the reception can enhance every guest's sense of the event as a Jewish community function, not just as a private family party. Your synagogue undoubtedly has an established system for handling Bar/Bat Mitzvah receptions and you can easily find out how things are done. You simply need to get in touch with the right person, the executive director, the president of the Sisterhood, or another member who has just held a similar Bar or Bat Mitzvah party.

The synagogue is not the only suitable place to hold a reception. But even if you plan to have a private party elsewhere, it is usually appropriate to have *kiddush* or an *oneg Shabbat* at the synagogue immediately after services. It gives the congregation an opportunity to share refreshments and to congratulate your child and family. If your group of invited guests is to go to another location, it is necessary that this be made clear on the invitation. In most cases, it will help if you've included a detailed set of directions to guide the guests from the synagogue to the reception location.

The party following the ceremony may be held at your home if you've sufficient space to accommodate all the guests. There is something especially nice about a reception at home, or in your garden, but be certain that you have enough space inside in case the weather doesn't cooperate. The use of a tent can make more space available and provide protection against unpredictable weather. If you are the open house, do-it-at-home type, a party at home will be very appealing. It's intimate, personal and probably less expensive. No middleman adds to the cost. You remain in control and order what you may need for food, drinks, and center-pieces. You may be able to return unused and unopened packages. Understandably, many people are concerned about holding the party at home. They wonder about the following questions. Is my house big enough? Are the stairs an obstacle to the very young and very old? Do I need to child-proof my rooms? Will I be working so hard that I cannot enjoy the party? Am I willing to be the general contractor renting dishes, ordering food, hiring help? Will I save money by doing it myself? A party at home is a personal decision. Some parents love the idea; others find it a big burden. It may be the perfect solution or just what you don't want. Be honest with yourself. Of course, if you hold the main Bar/Bat Mitzvah reception elsewhere, you can still have a smaller gathering at home during the course of the weekend.

Frequently, a Bar/Bat Mitzvah reception is held at a hotel. You may have a choice among different rooms which are suitable for your event. Frequently, walls in hotel party rooms are movable to make the room just the right size. A hotel is a full service reception site for it can include the catering, dishes, tables, waiters, parking which you may need. They may offer a package deal from wine to dessert, which you may be able to modify to your taste. You may find it convenient to house your out-of-town guests at the same hotel. However, there may be disadvantages in choosing a hotel for your event. The quality of their catering service may not be their strong point. Paper-thin folding doors may not be as soundproof as you would hope. In using a hotel, watch your expenses because liquor, taxes, and gratuities can be costly.

Clubs, party rooms in an apartment building, social halls, or historic houses offer other possible party places. You may want to consider renting space in the YMHA, a county or municipal building, country club, or the like. Even if you do not belong, a local club may allow the use of its facilities for a fee. They provide the space and you provide the party package—music, food, decorations, tables, chairs, etc. Before renting a spot for your Bar/Bat Mitzvah celebration, check for adequate parking, handicap accessibility, sufficient space, adequate heating and cooling for a crowd. Plan ahead. Read the details of the contract to see what is included. Be an informed consumer.

Serving the Food: A buffet versus a served meal, or how are you going to feed all those invited guests and still enjoy the celebration?

It is important to remember that wine for kiddush and a challah for the *motzi* is all that is needed for congregational fellowship after a service. Platters of challah and thimble shaped wine glasses are adequate. This usually is served on tables in the synagogue social hall and congregants stand up and help themselves. Whatever you do to expand your Bar/Bat Mitzvah reception is your choice.

If you are planning to offer more, you must decide how the food is to be served. This decision affects your choice of menu and vice versa. Deciding on the style of serving will help you plan the menu. Here are three suggestions:

- A buffet or self-service meal. Using this form, guests may either stand up and eat or return to place settings at tables.
- A served meal.
- Individual tables with place settings and platters of food.

A mix of two styles may involve a served main course, with waiters clearing dishes, and a buffet dessert table. It all depends on where you are, how much space you have, the number of guests, budget, and tone you wish to maintain.

More people can be served at a lower cost if you choose a buffet. This works well if there are many children, for it allows some coming and going. If you use this style, it is important to have enough serving centers so all guests can be fed within a reasonable amount of time. Long buffet lines are unpleasant and should be avoided. Determine whether you need two, three, or more serving stations to

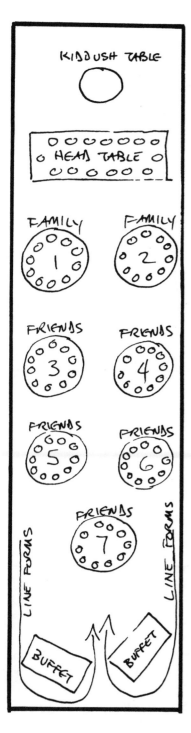

avoid bottlenecks. Consider the shape of the room, and then plan where to place the serving tables and how the lines should flow.

- An "X" in the middle of the room provides four separate self-service legs.
- A "U-shaped" table allows helpers to stand behind and serve your guests.
- Setting up two long straight buffet tables on opposite sides of the room provides another option.

A variation on the self-service theme is to have individual platters on each table so that guests can be seated and still serve themselves. This enables you to have large numbers of guests while serving them conveniently. A smoked fish or a delicatessen platter are among the menu selections suitable for this kind of setting. If you find that there is not enough room for all to be seated, reserve some of the available seating for the comfort of elderly guests.

A served meal is more formal, with a large part of the expense due to labor costs. To have a served meal may involve calling an established caterer who can handle most of the party details in addition to providing waiters, waitresses, kitchen help, and the like. If you want to be relieved of direct responsibility and the need to coordinate many details, you can call on a caterer who will have menu choices, rental equipment, and a price list for everything from flowers to tablecloths. They are in business to coordinate such an affair and using such a service is one option, but an expensive one. It is important to remember that a caterer's idea about how things are to be done may differ from yours. To avoid misunderstanding, you may want to write detailed instructions to specify how and when food is to be served and cleared. This leaves little to chance. You may have in mind an order of events such as prayers, speeches, songs, or toasts during the party, and your caterer should know about this ahead of time.

Planning the Menu

The menu is a matter of personal preference. It is influenced by those things that are unique about your child's Bar/Bat Mitzvah: your guest list, your date, relative costs, where and how your meal will be prepared. Realizing that the choices are endless and the combinations infinite, we are simply going to suggest some starting points.

There are many excellent Jewish cookbooks with ideas for planning a menu which fits your celebration and your pocketbook. If you choose to work with a caterer, remember that it is usually part of his service to offer suggestions for a well-rounded meal. Local delicatessens and some local supermarkets have printed lists of party platters and other ideas for feeding a large group of guests. You may also want to consider casseroles or something similar which can be cooked ahead and frozen in quantity. There will not be time for last minute food preparations, so plan accordingly. Of course, there is an interaction between planning the meal and serving the meal. Soup, for instance, may be difficult to serve from a buffet. So consider whether the meal will be buffet style or served when deciding on the menu.

Kiddush over wine is traditionally said at the meal following a joyful religious occasion. In selecting wine for the reception, it is appropriate to choose a kosher brand, whether it is from the United States or Israel. In fact, Conservative and Orthodox synagogues will insist that only kosher wine be used. Many liquor stores are willing to deliver an overestimated amount of wine and allow the return of unopened bottles. Sometimes they will provide you with a free case of glasses on loan as part of their service. Your synagogue may be able to supply wine glasses. Otherwise, you may rent glasses or buy plastic wine glasses. The latter are readily available from a party goods store.

Grape juice should be offered as well as wine. In every group, there are guests who prefer not to drink alcohol. Many of your guests are children who are legally underage. Within the bar/bat mitzvah circuit we have heard that some children try to take advantage of the availability of liquor. We suggest that you ask a friend to keep an eye on the situation so that children are not drinking alcohol left in half empty glasses or pouring wine into empty soda bottles. Also, ask someone to monitor the table where drinks are being served. Unfortunately, this problem must be taken seriously.

The Synagogue and Its Kitchen: Kashrut and a Mashgiach

When you plan the reception at your synagogue, your choices will be shaped by whether it has a kosher kitchen. If so, find out how your meal can conform to the dietary laws. Your congregation will probably have a list of appropriate caterers who may bring food into the synagogue. Some may allow strictly vegetarian caterers as well as approved kosher caterers. Usually, prepared foods may not be brought in from other sources. Otherwise, you may cook for your party in the synagogue kitchen. It may be necessary to hire a *mashgiach* to supervise the cooking. He is authorized by the rabbis of the community to see that food preparation complies with the dietary laws. Be sure to find out if there is a fee for his services.

Does your congregation allow anyone to heat its ovens on Shabbat? This can influence your choice of menu or the time for your reception. If it maintains *kashrut,* is your synagogue equipped to handle both meat and dairy meals? We know of one party consultant, who was proceeding well until she realized that a meat meal had been planned and the synagogue only had a dairy kitchen. Check ahead of time to avoid such problems.

Basic Checklist

You're going to need a lot of equipment to help serve your party guests. The list may include:

- Tables and chairs
- Tablecloths and napkins
- Plates
- Silverware
- Glasses

Your synagogue may be able to provide these items if you hold the party there, or you may secure them from a rental service, caterer, or a party goods store. Here, it is just a matter of personal taste and budget whether you select traditional china and silverware or disposable paper and plastic goods. If your synagogue or Sisterhood can provide most of these items, that probably will be the most economical solution. It would be appropriate and gracious to offer a donation in appreciation for the use of those items. If you elect one of the other options, you probably will find that the charges for renting dishes and the like come to only a bit more than using paper and plastic. If you do use disposable products, a few unobtrusive but strategically placed trash receptacles will simplify the table clearing process. If you choose to go with china and glasses not only will you have a rental fee to pay, but also you may need to hire help to clear away and wash the dishes at the end of the meal unless the rental service does its own washing.

Tables and chairs can be rented. To simplify matters try to rent everything from one place. It is not necessary to go as far as one woman who rented tables and chairs in Connecticut and tablecloths in New Jersey. Keeping rentals local and simple will avoid unnecessary driving and the extra difficulty of dealing with more than one company.

While lovely table settings are nice, remember that your guests gathering to celebrate is more important than any other concern. Whether you are setting up things yourself or having someone else do it for you, it is handy to have a master sheet of instructions so nothing is overlooked.

- First you may need an overall blueprint of the room.

    If your living room furniture needs to be moved and replaced by a rented buffet table, where does everything go?

    If you are using a social hall, where are the tables to be placed?

    Will there be a head table?

- Second, there should be specifics detailing what goes on each individual table.

    Tablecloth, napkins

    Dishes, silverware, glasses for wine and water

    Bottles of wine

    Flowers or other centerpiece

    Basket with rolls

    Condiments

    Birkat ha-Mazon booklets for reciting grace after the meal

    Other items

- Other possible tables for the following:

    Drinks

    Buffet dinner or dessert service

    Placecards

It's a good idea to duplicate these overall charts so that everyone who needs a copy can have one. On the day of the Bar/Bat Mitzvah, it will be helpful for a friend to have this information so that she can make sure that things have been done correctly. If a friend is willing to take on that responsibility you'll be free from those distracting concerns during the ceremony and celebration.

Flowers and Centerpieces

On its Bar/Bat Mitzvah weekend, the family may be expected to provide flowers for the synagogue *bimah*. There may be a regular procedure for ordering flowers, a certain florist, and a set amount of expenditure. The Sisterhood may be in charge of that function and may ask you for a donation so that the flowers are your gift in honor of the occasion. If you are interested and there is time, you may be able to specify the floral design. If your reception is at the synagogue, you may wish to order some coordinating flowers for the party area. Afterward, if you can move the sanctuary flowers to the reception, it will all look well planned. While individual floral centerpieces look lovely, they can add up in cost. To save money, some parents order loose flowers in bulk. Then, they or helpful friends make arrangements for each table. Other families have used silk flowers which may be less expensive. Often, one guest at each table gets to take home the centerpiece. A friend of ours had a different idea. Immediately after her reception, she sent her flowers to Children's Hospital to brighten its halls.

If you are providing tables for all your guests, you may want to consider other centerpiece options. These may reflect either the season of the year or a Jewish holiday that is near. In the fall near *Sukkot*, you may want to fill individual baskets with fruits of the season. At *Chanukah*, one could use a simple *Chanukiah* on each table. Sometimes a footed cake plate is used as a centerpiece with a colorful display of assorted desserts. In some communities it has become customary to place cans of food in an attractive display at the center of each table. After the party, this "arrangement" is donated to a food bank such as Mazon, a Jewish organization which feeds the hungry. Another unusual centerpiece has been suggested by Jewish librarians. You can place a small assortment of books with Jewish content on each table which can then be donated to your synagogue library. A variation on the book theme was done by a friend who wanted to share her Sephardic background. She found an historical novel which she used as a centerpiece. Guests took the books home and were able to read about the heritage of the bar/bat mitzvah family. Let your imagination and your budget dictate what can be done. Remember that something you plan and do yourself will be an original expression of your taste and will cost less than something done where others' labor is involved. Perhaps some friends or members of the congregation will be pleased to help you.

Music and Singing

First consult the ritual leaders of your congregation to learn your synagogue's customs relating to playing music at the time your reception will be held. The answer may range from the prohibition of playing music on Shabbat, until sundown, to a completely open range of choices for you. Knowing what is considered appropriate, you can then work out the details.

Above all, music at your Bar/Bat Mitzvah party should enhance the occasion, helping to express your joy at being Jewish and your happiness that your child has just been called to the Torah for the first time. What is Jewish music? In the *Encyclopedia Judaica*, Curt Sachs says, "Jewish music is that music which is made by Jews, for Jews, as Jews."[3] This definition reflects how broad Jewish music can be.

You may want to choose a folk singer, Klezmer music, a group that leads Israeli dancing or a composite tape of recorded music. Any of these choices will give your party a special Jewish flavor. Jewish music can be live or recorded, depending on the availability of musicians and your budget. See if your community has a Jewish folk arts society which lists these musicians. Otherwise, check at your synagogue, Jewish book stores or local Jewish newspaper. If you prefer, you might want to look into hiring a deejay or a live band. Usually, you can watch videos of different bands before making your choice. Alternatively, you can stop in at a party where they are performing to see them in person. Be sure to call the party host/hostess first. Before you sign the contract for any music, you may want to ask the following questions:

3. *Encyclopedia Judaica*, Volume 12 (Jerusalem, Israel: Keter Publishing, 1972), p. 555.

- How much are you willing to spend on music? Most people assume that bands cost more than deejays, but some disc jockeys can be very costly.
- Will the specific entertainers you previewed be those coming to your party? See if you can specify names of performers in your contract. One family found that their entire original troupe had made *aliyah* before the Bar/Bat Mitzvah.
- What is the right size musical group for your room and for your number of guests?
- Will your deejay try to take complete control of your party by running non-stop activities or games?
- How long will music play and how long with the breaks be?
- Can you select specific songs?
- Do you want music played while your guests are eating? Both style and volume are important, for overly loud music may drown out conversation.
- What extra charges might come up—overtime, feeding the band, taxes, favors?

If your synagogue does not permit musical instruments on Shabbat, there are many vocalists who are eager to teach Jewish songs and Israeli dancing to your guests as part of their presentation. This participation adds a warm Jewish dimension to the celebration and is always appropriate. Even without additional musical background, it is possible to include group singing as part of the festivities. It will be helpful to provide song sheets which have words in Hebrew and Yiddish, as appropriate, and in transliteration where needed, to give everyone a chance to be part of the group singing. In any of these ways, this form of Jewish music can enhance the atmosphere of your Bar/Bat Mitzvah party.

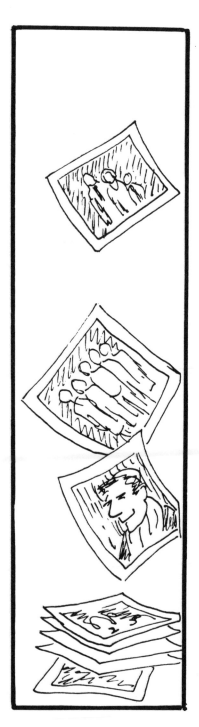

Photography, and other ways to preserve memories

Photographs help preserve memories of the Bar/Bat Mitzvah. First, check your synagogue's policy about photography at the ceremony and reception. Most likely, photography is not permitted during the ceremony for it would disturb the service. Therefore, to capture this important moment on film, a better course is to stage photos on the *bimah* ahead of the actual date. If you know certain guests are avid amateur photographers, you'll want to mention this prohibition in advance to avoid any awkward moments on the Bar/Bat Mitzvah day. To put matters in a more positive light, you could ask such a guest to bring his equipment to record events that take place after the synagogue ceremony. If this person is primarily responsible for the photographic record of the Bar/Bat Mitzvah, encourage him to include everyone in the pictures, not just those guests he knows. Otherwise, as has happened, you may be overwhelmed with snapshots of his side of the family to the exclusion of the rest of your Bar/Bat Mitzvah party. By calling on a guest to be the photographer, you are gaining a permanent record without the expense of hiring a professional. Undoubtedly, you have a friend or relative who would be delighted to take pictures.

If having a professional job is important to you, then ask friends to back-up your hired photographer. Years after the event, photos will bring back wonderful memories. To find a suitable professional, get firsthand recommendations from experienced bar/bat mitzvah parents. Your photographer should be someone who:

- Is experienced with the bar/bat mitzvah reception and therefore able to anticipate its important moments.
- Has good references and a portfolio of his work for you to see.
- Blends in with your guests, so that his work is inobtrusive.
- Knows how to deal with kids.

With today's technology, there are other ways to capture the Bar/Bat Mitzvah experience for posterity. Some families, whose personal degree of observance permits, use a video-cassette recorder at their reception. Another option is to use a recording device at the synagogue service if this is permitted. If your synagogue uses a microphone and amplification at the ceremony, it may be possible to tap into the public address system with a recording device. Having the service recorded on tape gives you a vivid and meaningful remembrance of that day's experiences. If you are not particularly capable in this field, a friend or audio consultant may be able to help you set up an unobtrusive recording arrangement. Of course, first ask your rabbi if this will be acceptable.

Cost-Cutting Hints

- You will save money if food is ordered in bulk, and later arranged on platters.
- If friends volunteer to prepare something for your reception, accept their offers. That will leave less for you to handle yourself.
- Friends and other Bar/Bat Mitzvah parents may join together to help you cook and bake for your *simcha*. This can be done in small batches at home and put into individual freezers.
- Kosher catering is usually expensive. One family we know gathered friends to cook in large quantities in their own synagogue's kitchen. This was done, under supervision, in accordance with the laws of *kashrut*.
- Check for discounts when feeding young children. Caterers often have a separate scale for those under 12.
- Can you buy the wine and liquor yourself rather than having the caterer bring it? This can save you money. Check to see if the merchant will allow you to return unopened bottles for full credit. Also ask the merchant if he offers the free use of wine glasses as part of his service. Free delivery and pick-up may also be included which saves you both time and effort.
- Be your own party planner to save money and to keep the celebration under your control. Talk to friends who have already had bar/bat mitzvahs for ideas.
- Some congregations call upon the parents to help with receptions during the year of their child's bar/bat mitzvah. This cooperative labor pool offsets the extra expense of hiring help. You might consider suggesting this to your fellow bar/bat mitzvah parents.
- Friends of ours joined together to found a dish cooperative where they purchased flatware and glassware for 200. Each of 15 families chipped in approximately $150.00. They all use the dishes when their individual *simchas* occur. If you can put together such a group, you will save significant amounts of money in the long run.
- Help may be needed for serving, clearing dishes, and cleaning up. Some friends, college students, or members of the synagogue maintenance staff may be able to assist you at lower expense than professional help.
- In lieu of renting plates, silverware, and other party accessories, consider paper and plastic goods. They may cost less when all factors are considered, including rental charges, breakage, and fees for help.
- One family holding an outdoor reception avoided the whole issue of serving platters and place settings. Instead, they prepared individual meals inside corsage boxes which were distributed to guests.
- If you want colorful tablecloths, rather than renting them, it may be possible to buy yards of inexpensive, easy-care, bright fabric or sheets which you can

make into tablecloths yourself. Afterward you may keep them for your own use or you may donate them to the synagogue for use by others.

- Making your own centerpiece can let you realize savings. You may create centerpieces which also serve as part of the meal, such as bowls of fruit or trays of petit fours.
- It may be possible to order flowers in bulk and you and your friends can make the individual arrangements. This allows quite a savings in labor costs.
- Holding your reception at the synagogue is not only in keeping with the tone of the day, but usually is less expensive than renting a commercial facility.

Ideas for Providing for Your Youngest Guests

- Some families offer children a separate menu; others offer children basically the same meal as adults. Consider the ages and usual tastes of younger guests before deciding what to offer them. This can help you avoid waste.
- At a seated reception, it may be wise to have guests sit as families so that parents are at each table to supervise their own young children. Older children may have a table of their own.
- If you hire a baby-sitter, it may be a good idea to have the sitter available during the reception as well as the service. Remember that the sitter will need a meal if she stays this long.
- Buffet service allows some mobility and is less formal than a served meal. This self-service style may be more suitable if you are inviting a large number of children.
- Children sometimes like to have a party for their own friends. This may be done at a later date, perhaps in cooperation with other Bar/Bat Mitzvah children. In this way, you can share expenses.

NOTES:

Gifts:
Giving and
Receiving

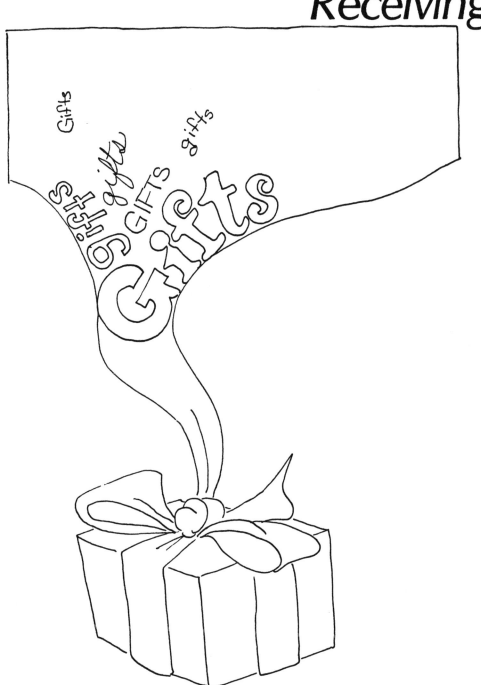

Gifts: Giving and Receiving

Gifts given to a Bar/Bat Mitzvah child should be selected with the understanding that a Bar/Bat Mitzvah is not the same as a birthday party for a thirteen-year-old. It is a religious occasion marking a passage in the Jewish life cycle. One should not think just in terms of a suitable birthday present, but rather of something which reflects the special character of the day. As a parent, you may be asked to make suggestions. What are appropriate gifts with Jewish meaning? Here are some ideas.

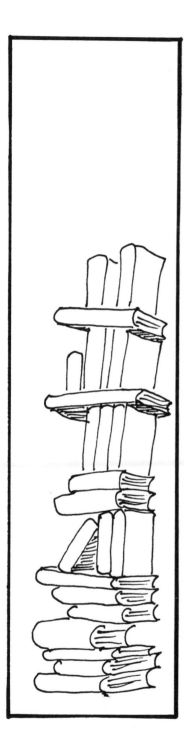

Gifts with Jewish Meaning

● Books on Jewish Topics

Having a personal Jewish library has always been a priority in our tradition, whether one has only a few volumes or considerably more. Jews long have been known as "the people of the book," oriented to the written records of our heritage. A book makes a most appropriate gift for a Bar/Bat Mitzvah child. What specific books make good Bar/Bat Mitzvah presents?

A prayer book, referred to as a *siddur*.

A Bible or *Chumash*, which is the Torah printed in book form. This comes in various translations, with or without commentaries and parallel Hebrew verses.

Other primary Jewish sources such as individual volumes of books of Samuel, Isaiah, Ecclesiastes, or Job.

Scholarly commentaries that analyze Jewish writings. For example, Maimonides, Rashi, Nehama Leibowitz, and many, many others.

Books on Jewish history, ethics, and traditions. There are single and multivolume encyclopedias written on a level suitable for a Bar/Bat Mitzvah child. For example, *The Junior Judaica,* c/o Maccabee Publishing Co., 14 W. Forest Ave., Englewood, N.J. 07631.

Biographies of famous Jews.

Books about the state of Israel—history, archaeology, natural history, some which emphasize a pictorial approach.

Always popular gifts are *The Jewish Catalog,* Volumes I, II, and III; *Jewish Chronicles,* a three volume set; and Martin Gilbert's *Jewish History Atlas* and *Jerusalem History Atlas.*

An easy way to select books is from the mail-order offerings of Jewish book clubs and publishing houses. The following list is by no means all-inclusive:

Jewish Book Club
834 North 12th Street
Allentown, PA 18102
FAX (215) 437-2165

Jewish Publication Society
1930 Chestnut Street
Philadelphia, PA 19103
(215) 564-5925

UAHC Publications
858 Fifth Avenue
New York, NY 10021
(212) 249-0100

United Synagogue Book Service
155 Fifth Avenue
New York, NY 10010
(212) 533-7800

Behrman House
235 Watchung Avenue
West Orange, NJ 07052
(800) 221-2755
Behrman offers a large selection of Jewish bestsellers, classics, history, theology, fiction, reference, Bible and prayer books with an especially good selection for children.

Jonathan David Company
68-22 Eliot Avenue
Middle Village, NY 11379
(718) 894-2818
FAX (718) 894-2818
A large Judaica book guide with over 60 pages of interesting books.

Ma'ayan Book Company
P.O. Box 3197
Framingham, MA 01701
(800) 262-2926
The "one stop shopping" for all your Judaica book needs.

America's Jewish Bookstore
The Catalog For A Jewish Lifestyle
(800)-JUDAISM
Fax: (412) 421-6103
(In Canada call 800-776-9545)
This extensive catalog features books, records, and tapes. When you call, ask them about the Jewish ritual items which they also stock.

And a suggestion for those who have entered the computer age:

Judaic Software Gift Catalog
Davka Corporation
7074 N. Western Avenue
Chicago, IL 60645
(800) 621-8227
Davka specializes in Jewish software for the Macintosh and the IBM PCs. You will have access to the Tanakh, the Babylonian Talmud, Rashi texts and others via computer programs. They also offer programs with Hebrew lettering, on-line Jewish calendars, and Hebrew language programs. There is also a Jewish version of HyperCard called Otzar Plus and a Hebrew version of Microsoft Windows called HaKotev or Dagesh.

• Jewish Ritual Items
Ritual objects have a timeless quality and they make wonderful gifts. They can be used in religious ceremonies throughout the weekly and yearly cycle of Jewish celebration. Your Jewish bookstore, Judaica or synagogue shop should stock most of these ritual objects and may be willing to fill telephone orders. Suggested items include:

Tallit with tallit bag	Tefillin and tefillin bag
Kiddush cup	Shabbat candlesticks
Challah cover	Seder plate
Menorah	Spice box

The stores listed below are willing to fill telephone or mail orders:

Hamakor Gallery
4150 W. Dempster
Skokie, IL 60076
(708) 677-4150

In the Spirit
460 East 79th St.
New York, NY 10021
(212) 861-5222
A studio/gallery specializing in new objects for old traditions.

Israeli Accents
4838 Boiling Brook Parkway
Rockville, MD 20852
(301) 231-7999
Discounted invitations and Judaica.

Avraham Yakin
P.O. Box 6271
Meyuhas Street #7
Jerusalem ISRAEL
011-972-2-389-097
An artist who offers original bar/bat mitzvah lithograph certificates with the individual information about the child filled in by calligraphy. These can be made and mailed on short notice directly to the bar/bat mitzvah.

Jewish mail-order catalogues fill an important need. Here are the names and phone numbers of such businesses:

California Stitchery
(800) 345-3332
(818) 781-9515
They specialize in Judaic stitchery kits of all kinds.

Galerie Robin
(800) 635-8279
(615) 356-8345
They carry a wide range of attractive Judaica.

Hamakor Judaica, Inc.
(800) 426-2567
FAX (708) 966-4033
Their extensive catalogue offers ritual items, gifts, art, books, etc.

Nefesh Ami: Soul of My People
(516) 933-2660
(516) 933-2196
They offer Judaica, while specializing in Jewish music.

Tara Publications
(516) 295-2290
FAX (516) 295-2291
They specialize in Jewish music: Israeli, Yiddish, Chasidic. Available items include tapes, CDs, and sheet music.

For The Children
8420 Bustle Avenue
Philadelphia, PA 19152
(800) 633-1518
This company specializes in gifts, novelties, books, games, kitchen products and jewelry for all occasions.

Unusual Jewish Gifts

● For something out of the ordinary:
You can order a bar/bat mitzvah scroll with the child's *Haftarah* portion in Hebrew and English. This "Simcha Scroll" is printed on parchment, personalized in calligraphy with the name of the honoree, the occasion, and the date. The parchment is scrolled into a 15″ carved hardwood case, a lucite display stand is included. For more information contact: Jerusalem Products Company, The Simcha Scroll, 33 Deer Run Drive, Randolph, NJ 07869; phone/fax: (201) 895-3231.

Your local Jewish Community Center or YMHA-YWHA may have a special membership for teens. This youth membership could be a fine Bar/Bat Mitzvah present. It offers a Jewish community connection to the child while helping support a local Jewish institution.

Another possibility is to offer to take the Bar/Bat Mitzvah child on a tour of American-Jewish historic interest. A trip to New York's Lower East Side and the Chasidic and other Orthodox communities in Brooklyn may leave a lasting impression on the youngster. These are places where Yiddish is still the everyday language, and hearing it on the lips of children no older than he is certain to put him in quick touch with his roots.

A Trip To Israel

A quality Israel experience is important in developing Jewish identity. It gives youngsters a creative way to express their Jewishness. Throughout the country, leaders from United Jewish Appeal, Charles R. Bronfman (CRB) Foundation, Council of Jewish Federations, Jewish Education Service of North America, area congregations and JCCs are striving to make a trip to Israel available for every Jewish teen. Currently, about 8,000 young people visit Israel annually and the goal is to increase that figure to 50,000. Quoted in *The New York Times* and *The Washington Jewish Week*, Charles Bronfman describes such trips as:

> a new rite of passage in the lives of young Jews. Walking the land of Israel, meeting its people and experiencing the culture . . . leaves a deep and enduring impression which can change the lives of North American Jewish youth.

Building an Israel travel fund for each child is a critical element. In certain communities, starting in elementary school, UJA, the parents, and the home congregation make payments into this fund annually. Another idea is to set up an Israel Fund at the time of bar/bat mitzvah. Instead of getting ten Nintendo games, your child will be registered for a trip to Israel. Guests will know they may give to a cooperative fund which will offer the bar/bat mitzvah a pivotal Israel experience.

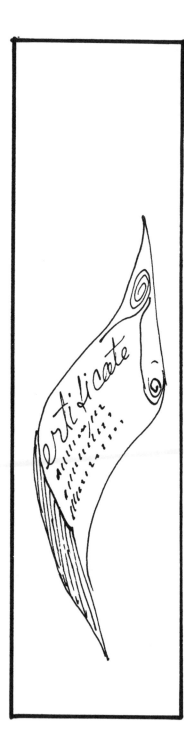

Tzedakah

The obligation to help the poor and needy is stated in the Bible and has been considered basic by Jewish leaders throughout the ages. Becoming a Bar/Bat Mitzvah, a young Jewish person has reached the age of responsibility for the *mitzvot.* Primary among these is *tzedakah,* a word difficult to translate for it means much more than charity. Rather it has a connotation of righteousness, the root being the same as in the Hebrew word *tzaddiks,* a righteous person. Within the context of gifts, how can this idea of *tzedakah* be transmitted to the Bar/Bat Mitzvah child?

Danny Siegel, an author, suggests how the Bar/Bat Mitzvah experience can include an exposure to the value of *tzedakah.* He feels that a child should be encouraged to donate a portion of the money he receives as gifts on this occasion. He may need instruction and guidance in selecting a worthy cause for this purpose. Now that the child has demonstrated his intention to take on adult religious responsibilities, giving *tzedakah* enables him to act upon this.

It is in the best Jewish tradition to make an offering to a community organization in honor of a *simcha* or joyous event. In lieu of a present for the child, guests may make charitable contributions in the child's name. Occasionally a family may decide that it prefers to receive no personal Bar/Bat Mitzvah gifts. The giving of *tzedakah* acknowledges that even while rejoicing, a Jew has concern for others. A charity of one's own choosing is perfectly appropriate. Usually the organization receiving the donation sends a card to the Bar/Bat Mitzvah child stating that a contribution was made in the child's honor. Here are some suggestions for a contribution:

- One can plant trees in Israel as a living gift. The Jewish National Fund and B'nai B'rith support reforestation projects. If you specify, trees can be designated for the John F. Kennedy, Martin Luther King, Challenger, or Holocaust Survivors Forest. Some of these forests offer a certificate which can be framed for the Bar/Bat Mitzvah child. In addition, the Jewish National Fund has a Bar/Bat Mitzvah book in Israel where the child's name and photograph can be permanently recorded. Please write to the Jewish National Fund (JNF) at 8607 Second Avenue, Suite 404-A, Silver Spring, MD 20910, or call (800) 345-8565.
- Contributions are welcomed by various institutions which support the Jewish community.

  United Jewish Appeal Federation of Greater Washington, 6101 Montrose Road, Rockville, MD 20852, (301) 230-7200 or your local Federation

  Hadassah, 50 West 58th Street, New York, NY 10019, (212) 355-7900

  Israel Bonds, 4733 Bethesda Avenue, Bethesda, MD 20814, (301) 654-6575

  Ziv Tzedakah Fund, 11818 Trail Ridge Drive, Potomac, MD 20854, (301) 279-2605.

- Project Chai: feeding hungry Jews in the former Soviet Union. Jews in Jewish communities of the ex-Soviet Union cannot afford to buy food. By sending food parcels via courier with a confirmed receipt, a bar/bat mitzvah can take responsibility for his people in need. You can make these arrangements through the Washington Committee for Soviet Jewry—Project Chai, 1401 Blair Mill Road, Silver Spring, MD 20910, (301) 587-4455.
- Twinning with an Ethiopian Jew. In order to support Ethiopian Jewry, the North American Conference on Ethiopian Jewry (NACOEJ) has established a special bar/bat mitzvah gift. The point is to help an American bar/bat mitzvah child share their coming-of-age with an Ethiopian boy or girl. Through this program, children in America and Ethiopian children in Israel make personal contact, exchange letters and photos and get to know one another. Twinning gives American youngsters a chance to begin their lives as religiously mature Jews by undertaking to help new Israelis get a good start in their lives. The gift made by the American bar/bat mitzvah goes not to the individual "twin" but to the "twin's" class or school so that many Ethiopian children may benefit. A minimum of $50.00 is the suggested amount for participation. For more information about this wonderful program contact NACOEJ, 165 E. 56th Street, N.Y., NY 10022, (212) 752-6340.
- The Society for Protection of Nature in Israel. This organization does many projects connected to beautifying the country. They also build and support the 25 Field Schools throughout Israel. A contribution of $36.00 will enroll

the bar/bat mitzvah in this worthy organization and they will receive a magazine about Israel. Contact SPNI, 25 West 45th, N.Y., NY 10036, (212) 389-6750.

We know some bar/bat mitzvah children who have generated their own personalized ideas for *tzedakah*:

- One child, who has worn glasses since the age of one, asked friends and relatives to honor her by making a contribution to the eye clinic of Hadassah Hospital in Israel.
- Another child, who had an interest in basketball, asked that guests make a contribution to the Ilan Sports Center in Israel which helps disabled children. This sports center also helps train children for the Special Olympics.
- One young man, whose Torah reading told the story of Noah, asked for contributions to be made to the Biblical Zoo in Jerusalem where the zoo maintains two of every animal mentioned in the Bible.
- One boy with a keen interest in nature asked that he be honored with contributions to the Society for Protection of Nature in Israel. The contributions made in his honor went towards paying for a brochure about the area around the Northern Galilee.

With your encouragement, your child could find an organization which appeals to his own interests and which will enable him to share with those less fortunate.

Underscoring the importance of *tzedakah*, Danny Siegel offers a novel thought. He suggests that a parent estimate the cost of the Bar/Bat Mitzvah including the party. Using this as the basis, calculate an amount for *tzedakah*. You can add a percentage above the estimated cost or cut back on some anticipated expense, such as flowers or favors, and allocate that amount as a donation. MAZON: A Jewish Response to Hunger points out that "our ancestors left the corners of their fields for the needy. You can follow in their footsteps by sending MAZON 3% of the cost of your celebration." Their national office is 2940 Westwood Blvd., Suite 7, Los Angeles, CA 90064-4102, (310) 470-7769. In a world where so many are in need, the bar/bat mitzvah is a perfect opportunity for sharing with others. Other agencies which help the poor, hungry and ill include:

American Friends of Lifeline for the Old in Israel, 1500 Palisades Avenue, Fort Lee, NJ 07024, (201) 947-2140.

Dorot, 171 West 85th Street, New York, NY 10025, (212) 769-2850.

Long Island Cares, Inc., P.O. Box 1073, West Brentwood, NY 11717, (516) 435-0454.

National Institute for Jewish Hospice, 8723 Alden Drive, Los Angeles, CA 90048, (213) 854-3036.

Remembering Your Synagogue

In many communities, it is customary to make a contribution to your synagogue in honor of the bar/bat mitzvah. This gift recognizes that the congregation provided a religious education for your child, role models for Jewish identity and professional training for the bar/bat mitzvah ceremony. At this time, it may also be fitting to give an honorarium to your rabbi, cantor, tutor and other professionals who gave you special assistance. The bar/bat mitzvah offers a wonderful time to support Jewish leadership and institutions which link the community from generation to generation.

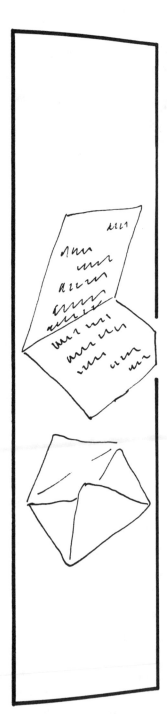

The Thank You Note: Taking the time to respond properly and promptly

A Bar or Bat Mitzvah gift is an expression of caring. Often the present has been thoughtfully selected by a close friend or relative. As a result, the bar/bat mitzvah can show his caring by responding promptly and graciously with a thank you note. The process of handling the gifts and thank you notes often involves some parental guidance. Children of age twelve and thirteen are still learning and parents can help them.

It is useful to keep records of all gifts. The gift should be listed with the name of the person who gave it, the date of arrival, and the date of acknowledgment. In the "Charts and Timetables Section," there is a sample chart for recording this information. Thanking people is the responsibility of the child, part of growing up through the Bar/Bat Mitzvah process. Different children will need varying levels of supervision depending on their motivation, personal standards, and spelling ability. A thank you note need not be a masterpiece, but it should demonstrate care in its preparation.

General guidelines for your child:

- Address the people appropriately. Whether he's writing to Aunt Sarah or Mr. and Mrs. Feldman, the name should be written in the proper form and spelled correctly.
- Be quite specific about the gift. A mimeographed note is unacceptable and so is "thank you for the gift."
- The thank you note should be sent within a few weeks. It is embarrassing to receive a call asking if the gift ever arrived. Avoid this by making sure that notes go out in a timely fashion.

NOTES:

Alternatives
for the Ceremony
and Celebration

Alternatives for the Ceremony and Celebration

Options: Israel, Bat Torah, Retreat Center, Adult Bar/Bat Mitzvah

Judaism is a community based religion. Many of its commandments deal with relationships between people, for a person leads a Jewish life in relation to others. Judaism is not a religion of withdrawal nor of isolated spirituality. Therefore, it follows that a bar/bat mitzvah child stands before a congregation to proclaim his intention to lead a responsible Jewish life. While most families hold the ceremony in their synagogue, some prefer to go to Israel, to use their home, a retreat center, a social hall or other alternative sites.

While Bar/Bat Mitzvah at age thirteen is more common, other possibilities include the Bat Torah ceremony for Orthodox girls or an adult Bar/Bat Mitzvah.

MASADA

A
HEIGHT
IN
JEWISH
HISTORY

Holding the Ceremony in Israel: The Kotel (Western Wall), Atop Masada, or Elsewhere

Since the establishment of the state of Israel, some people have chosen to travel to Israel with close family and friends to hold the Bar or Bat Mitzvah there. Israelis welcome children coming to celebrate in their land. Your family could even be invited to attend a reception at the home of the president of Israel to honor children who have come to Israel to mark their coming of age. Having the ceremony in Israel links two underlying strands in Jewish tradition, identification with one's people and love of Zion. For some families, a trip to Israel is a dream which they realize at the time of their child's Bar/Bat Mitzvah. With the reunification of Jerusalem in 1967, a boy may now have his Bar Mitzvah at the Kotel, the Western Wall of the Temple Mount. Another popular setting is Masada, a symbol of freedom and hope for the Jewish people since the time of the Romans. On a Monday or Thursday morning, a group departs for Masada and ascends to its summit. A Sefer Torah is brought along with the group as it leaves from Jerusalem. The Bar Mitzvah service takes place there amidst the ruins of an ancient synagogue atop the citadel. After the ceremony (and there may be more than one), the day of touring continues.

To have a Bar/Bat Mitzvah in Israel, boys should be thirteen according to the Hebrew calendar and girls at least twelve. While you will find opportunities for a bat mitzvah in many settings in Israel, be sure to check local customs.

The Reform and Conservative Movements offer help in arranging a Bar/Bat Mitzvah in Israel. An interested family should begin planning at least six months ahead or even earlier for a summer date. For an overview of options, contact:

- Association of Reform Zionists of America (ARZA)
  838 Fifth Avenue, New York, NY 10021
  (212) 249-0100
- World Council of Conservative/Masorti Synagogues
  155 Fifth Avenue, New York, NY 10010
  (212) 533-7693
  To call Israel directly, dial 011 (international access)—972 (country, Israel) then the numbers listed below.
- Center for Conservative Judaism in Israel
  2 Agron Street, P.O. Box 7456, Jerusalem, Israel
  Tel: 2-256-386   Fax: 2-234-127
- Israel Movement for Progressive Judaism, Hebrew Union College/Jerusalem Campus,
  13 King David Street, Jerusalem, Israel
  Fax: 2-203446

In Israel, here are some smaller congregations which may welcome your bar or bat mitzvah service.

- Beit Daniel, Tel Aviv, 3-544-2740
- Har El, 16 Shmuel Hanagid Street, Jerusalem, 2-253-841
- Kol Ha Neshama, 57 Harakevet Street, Jerusalem 2-731-201
- Leo Baeck, 90 Derech Zarfa Street, Haifa, 4-331-080
- Ramat Zion, 68 Bar Kochba Street, French Hill, Jerusalem, 2-816-303

Other official agencies offer assistance. United Jewish Appeal has a Summer Family Mission which is scheduled four times each summer. It is a multi-generational tour geared to extended families travelling together. The participants pay but the bar/bat mitzvah child is free. UJA also offers a tour for singles incorporating a bar/bat mitzvah as well as an adult bar/bat mitzvah in Israel for those who have not had this experience. One can go anytime but most go during the summer. Participation does not require a contribution nor is it subsidized. All UJA bar/bat mitzvah ceremonies take place atop Masada. You can contact UJA directly at 99 Park Avenue, New York, NY 10016, (212) 818-9100. The state of Israel itself seeks to facilitate bar/bat mitzvah travel. To get detailed information, call El Al Israel's Airline, the Israeli Embassy or Consulate, or the Israel Government Tourist Office, 350 Fifth Avenue, New York, NY 10118—(212) 560-0600, extension 245.

You can turn to a travel agent who offers a packaged tour or a personalized itinerary. Here are six companies which have been recommended to us. Some offer a program where the bar/bat mitzvah child goes free if accompanied by a minimum number of paying participants.

- Tova Gilead, Inc., 199 Curtis Road, Hewlett Neck, NY 11598, (800) 242-TOVA, Fax (212) 629-0417
- Israel Travel Advisory Service, Inc. (ITAS), 18 Canoe Brook Drive, Livingston, NJ 07039, (800) 326-ITAS, Fax (201) 535-3368.
- Israel Discovery Tours, 30 Robert Frost Road, Sudbury, MA 01776, (800) 253-1553, Fax (508) 443-2423
- Ayelet Tours, Ltd., 21 Aviation Road, Albany, NY (800) 237-1517, (518) 437-0695
- Israel Identity Tours, 10324 Bells Mill Terrace, Potomac, MD 20854, (301) 299-6980
- Margaret Morse Tours, 17070 Collins Avenue, Suite 262, Miami Beach, FL 33160, (800) 327-3191

Additional companies advertise in the Jewish press, *The New York Times* and other major newspapers.

These companies offer a bar/bat mitzvah tour which is totally set so that there are few decisions to make. As a supplement to the bar/bat mitzvah ceremony, their package may include special highlights such as jeep travel in the desert or a visit to a new air force museum in Beersheva. If you prefer to travel independently, you can make individualized plans for your lodging, ceremony and reception.

Whatever you have in mind for a bar/bat mitzvah in Israel, start planning far in advance. Since international mails can be slow and unreliable, you may want to telephone or to fax. In addition, you may with to locate a contact person in Israel who will act as your go-between for any arrangements which you or your travel agent cannot handle on your own. If this person is not a good friend or relative, you may be asked to pay a fee for these services. People offering this assistance usually can be found by word-of-mouth. In any event, certain details will have to be handled after your arrival. However, we must emphasize that your child should be prepared for his part in the service well ahead of time as for any bar/bat mitzvah ceremony. Be sure to verify the Torah portion since there are several times a year when the portion read in Israel differs from the one read outside of Israel.

BAR/BAT
MITZVAH

IN JERUSALEM

FILLING IN

HISTORY

Although a Bar/Bat Mitzvah ceremony is symbolic of acceptance into the worldwide Jewish community, special consideration should be given to your own particular congregation. Having a Bar or Bat Mitzvah in Israel can be a beautiful and moving experience, but in addition, you may wish to hold a small ceremony at your own synagogue. In fact, your home congregation may offer special prayers upon your departure for Israel or upon your return. To connect the Israel experience with the American congregation, families often sponsor an *oneg shabbat* in honor of the Bar/Bat Mitzvah. At religious school, the bar/bat mitzvah child can share his Israeli experience by making a presentation and/or by showing a videotape of the event. This will give his friends a chance to be part of the celebration and to learn about Israel.

Bat Torah

Some synagogues do not offer the Bat Mitzvah ceremony at all; it is not included in their interpretation of Jewish law or tradition. So, in some cases, a Jewish girl simply does not experience a service marking this point in her life. On the other hand, some Jewish families who wish to acknowledge the religious achievements of their daughters have developed alternative ceremonies for this purpose. Perhaps the girl will give a meaningful speech or lead a learned discussion on the week's Torah portion. This discourse is called a *d'var* Torah. Or a girl may read Ecclesiastes during *Sukkot*, the *Megillah* of Esther during *Purim*, or the Book of Ruth at *Shavuot*, portions of the *Ketuvim*, the sacred writings, not from the Torah itself. The ceremony may be held at home, at a Jewish community center, or in a *sukkah* at that festive season if the synagogue is not a feasible setting for this religious event. Even though held outside the synagogue, this rite of passage is sometimes termed a Bat Mitzvah. Other times, it is referred to as a Bat Torah, suggesting that the girl has now publicly affirmed that she is a "daughter of the Torah." This has slightly different connotations from the term Bat Mitzvah and reflects that the girl has demonstrated her intention to follow the teachings of her Jewish heritage but avoids the suggestion that she is subject to exactly the same commandments as her brothers.

Nontraditional Settings

Judaism has always been a religion with great variety in its beliefs and its practices. In contrast to the usual synagogue-based Bar/Bat Mitzvah ceremony, other forms have developed that do without the synagogue entirely. In many instances, the atmosphere is strictly informal, whether it be at the Jewish community center or on a retreat.

Another new trend in American Judaism is to celebrate a child's bar/bat mitzvah at home. Those wishing to hold the ceremony at home point out that family celebrations such as seder and Shabbat dinner are home-based.

Here the emphasis is on an innovative and personalized experience. The intention is to be nontraditional, often with the parents structuring the ritual without the involvement of a rabbi. Prayers and songs may be done in a folk-rock idiom. We know of instances where readings included poetry written by the child, selections from Albert Einstein or Kahlil Gibran, along with portions from standard Jewish prayer. The Bar/Bat Mitzvah child may express his achievements by playing the flute or violin.

To hold such a nontraditional service, one would need a *minyan* of ten persons for the prayer service and a Torah scroll from which to read. Securing a Torah for your purposes may take some effort but it can be done. Some synagogues may be willing to loan a Torah, with a donation expected as a thank you. In lieu of borrowing large numbers of prayer books, many families prefer to create and print their own booklet for the service. One family, with both Jewish and non-Jewish relatives, held a *Havdalah* ceremony in a hotel. They did not have a rabbi; however, two young, knowledgeable women led the ceremony. They selected readings from the prayer book, poetry, and philosophy including authors such as Martin Buber, Martin Luther King, Shel Silverstein, and Elie Wiesel, compiling a totally original service. Their booklet was black and white, spiral bound, 8½" × 11", illustrated, with Hebrew, English and transliterations.

Another family with a thirteen year old boy and twelve year old girl chose to do something a little out of the ordinary, a Sunday, *Rosh Hodesh,* double ceremony. They had a particularly close friendship with another Jewish family who lived directly across the street. The friends opened up their home as a setting for the service. The children's aunt, a rabbi from Texas, officiated. This enabled the bar/bat mitzvah family to have their home set up for the festive meal which followed. At the conclusion of the service, the guests walked across the street. For further information about alternative Bar/Bat Mitzvah celebrations, consult *The Second Jewish Catalog,* pages 68–75.

Of the families seeking a nontraditional format for their child's Bar/Bat Mitzvah, many may not belong to a synagogue or may be members of an unaffiliated congregation, which is not part of the Reform, Conservative, Reconstructionist, or Orthodox movements. Others may belong to an institution which simply provides a school for the children, but no sanctuary for common worship. The Bar/Bat Mitzvah ceremony is viewed as an event which expresses personal feelings about coming of age within Judaism. They seek to create a celebration to convey this message. It becomes an event outside the traditional framework of American Judaism.

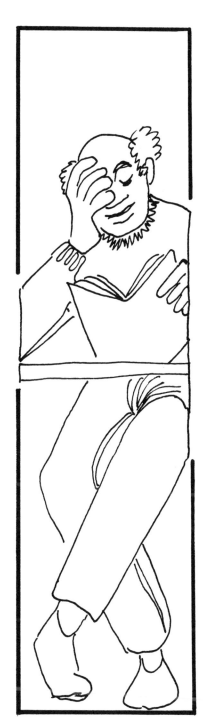

The Adult Bar/Bat Mitzvah

While this book is directed to preparing a child for a Bar or Bat Mitzvah, this ceremony need not occur at age thirteen. For those who have not had the opportunity, it is never too late to affirm publicly one's commitment to Judaism. Thousands and thousands of Jewish children have passed age thirteen without experiencing a Bar/Bat Mitzvah ceremony to mark the occasion. Often inspired by their own children's Jewish studies, men are participating in a belated ceremony. One boy in New York began his quest for his Jewish identity at age thirteen after his nonobservant parents completely ignored his religious education. This particular child, who had been so uncomfortable with Jewish ritual that he had not attended a friend's Bar Mitzvah, sought to learn more about his own background. Beginning a two-year course of study at a synagogue, he chose to have a Bar Mitzvah ceremony at the age of fifteen.

Some women who did not have an opportunity to prepare for this occasion may feel that something is lacking in their Jewish background. Some saw their brothers learn and grow through the Bar Mitzvah process and wished they could have had a similar experience. Seeking a firm identification with their Jewish heritage, these adult women today are preparing for a delayed Bat Mitzvah ceremony. Women of all ages, young professionals as well as grandmothers, have worked together and attained a strong sense of pride through this symbolic act.

Many congregations now are conducting an extended study program of Hebrew, rituals, Jewish history, and ethics, culminating in an adult Bar/Bat Mitzvah. Often this is a group experience with participation in the service shared by those completing the course of study. The Torah and *Haftarah* readings may be divided among those being honored as "sons and daughters of the commandments." If you are interested in starting an adult Bar/Bat Mitzvah program at your synagogue, you probably can find a like-minded group of adults with whom to study. Another possibility is for young adults, often of college age, to reach this goal with the guidance of a Hillel House, chavurah group, or the like. If this is something which appeals to you, we're confident that you will find the necessary support to achieve this goal.

Some people are fortunate enough to have a second Bar Mitzvah. In some congregations, it is customary to recognize a person of age eighty-three as a Bar Mitzvah, calling him to the Torah for an *aliyah* and possibly having him chant the *Haftarah*. Having reached age eighty-three, he is understood to have lived his normal, biblically appointed life span of seventy years and now is marking age thirteen again. Thus, appropriately, there is a second Bar Mitzvah ceremony.

NOTES:

Charts and Timetables

Bar/Bat Mitzvah Timetable:
Countdown to a Simcha*

Date Completed	EIGHTEEN MONTHS
	• Select a DATE • Find out your child's TORAH and HAFTARAH PORTION • Determine TUTORIAL arrangements to begin about nine months ahead
	ONE YEAR: PLAN THE BROAD OUTLINES OF YOUR CELEBRATION.
	• RECEPTION FACILITY—if not at the synagogue, reserve elsewhere. • FOOD—caterer, homemade, synagogue kitchen, or a combination. • MUSIC for a Jewish celebration.

*We have left sufficient space in the countdown so that you may fill in personal notes.

Date Completed	NINE MONTHS: PREPARE FOR THE CEREMONY
	• Find out what the child may do at BAR/BAT MITZVAH CEREMONY. • Child begins preparation for BAR/BAT MITZVAH PORTION.
	SIX MONTHS
	• Begin planning your GUEST LIST, using the charts at the back of this book. • If you will have a HAND-DESIGNED INVITATION, start planning for this. • Select TALLIT and TEFILLIN for your son.

BAR/BAT MITZVAH TIMETABLE: (cont'd)

Date Completed	FOUR MONTHS
	• ORDER INVITATIONS for delivery within four weeks. Take envelopes home, if possible. • RESERVE a block of hotel/motel rooms for out-of-town guests or arrange for HOST FAMILIES • Order KIPOT and/or SONG and PRAYER BOOKLETS.
	THREE MONTHS
	• Check availability of PARTY EQUIP-MENT: chairs, tables, linens, silverware, dishes. Arrange rental, if necessary. • Review GUEST LISTS.

BAR/BAT MITZVAH TIMETABLE: (cont'd)

Date Completed	TEN WEEKS
	• Determine your final GUEST LIST. • ADDRESS ENVELOPES.
	TWO MONTHS
	• Mail OUT-OF-TOWN INVITATIONS, including inserts for hotel or host-family arrangements and directions. • Complete plans for MEALS, either with caterer, your own cooking, or the assistance of friends. • Order CENTERPIECES for synagogue service and reception. • Engage ADDITIONAL HELP, if needed. • Prepare list of ALIYOT. Give instructions to those being honored.

BAR/BAT MITZVAH TIMETABLE: (cont'd)

Date Completed	SIX WEEKS
	• Mail LOCAL INVITATIONS. • Think about SEATING ARRANGE-MENTS. • Make up packet of LOCAL INFOR-MATION for out-of-town guests.
	THREE WEEKS
	• Arrange for a dress REHEARSAL in your synagogue for your child. • Make PLACECARDS.

BAR/BAT MITZVAH TIMETABLE: (cont'd)

Date Completed	THE LAST WEEK
	• Complete ALIYOT list and give copy to synagogue. • Time for FINAL REVIEW, if needed: —Hotel/motel or host families —Musician —Florist —Sufficient party equipment to accommodate guests —Food and wine —Additional help • Prepare a FRUIT BASKET, cheese platter, or sweets for hotel guests.

Preliminary Family List*

Date _____

	Father's Side	Mother's Side
Grandparents		
Great-aunts and Great-uncles		
Aunts and Uncles		

*Think of both local and out-of-town relatives. If you list one aunt, then all persons of a similar relationship should probably be included. Grandparents should contribute the names of relatives from each side.

163

Preliminary Family List

	Father's Side	Mother's Side
Parents' First Cousins		
Children of Parents' First Cousins		
Steprelatives		
Other Relatives		

Preliminary List of Friends of the Parents*

Date _____

Father's Friends	
Mother's Friends	
Grandparents' Friends	

*Local friends will know about the Bar/Bat Mitzvah through the grapevine. Groups of friends who know each other should be considered together. Think of close out-of-town friends who may want to make the effort to come or who would be offended if not invited. Think also of friends who know your child and would be proud to share this moment.

Preliminary List of Your Child's Friends*

Date _____

Children:
    From school, the neighborhood,
        religious school, camp, sports,
        scouting, etc.

Adults:
    Teachers and others.

*Think of your child's good friends. Ask your child to mention adults whom he wishes to include. He may want his piano teacher, some people for whom he baby-sits, or other adults he knows in special ways.

Preliminary List of Members of Your Congregation*

Date _____

Friends from within the Congregation

Regular Synagogue Attendees

---

*The size of this list depends on the nature of your congregation and your involvement with it. Through the years, you have come to know certain families through membership in your synagogue. In addition, many congregations have members who come regularly for Shabbat services. They may be at your Bar/Bat Mitzvah in any event. If you know them and numbers permit, you may want to honor them individually with an invitation so each feels welcome to share this day with you as an invited guest.

Preliminary List of Professional and Business Associates*

Date _____

Father's Business/Professional Associates	
Mother's Business/Professional Associates	

*If you wish to include associates, it is important to invite all those who fall into a similar category to avoid offending while you are trying to be gracious. But resist the temptation to turn this into a double-duty affair, thereby making a Bar/Bat Mitzvah celebration a big social gathering for your business friends.

Preliminary List of Neighbors*

Date _____

Neighbors	

*Immediate neighbors will certainly know that a Bar Mitzvah is forthcoming. However, you may not be able to invite the entire neighborhood. You should feel comfortable wherever you draw the line.

Final Guest List*

Guests	No.		Invited to:					DATE INVITATION MAILED	HOTEL/HOST	DIRECTIONS	LETTER	RS VP	No. Coming				THANK YOU NOTE
NAME AND ADDRESS	ADULTS	CHILDREN	FRI. DINNER	FRI. EVENING	SAT. MORNING	SAT. P.M. PARTY	SUNDAY BRUNCH					YES/NO	ADULTS	CHILDREN	ALIYAH	GIFT	

*You may need additional copies of this page depending on the size of your guest list.

Aliyot and Honors Chart*

For Bar/Bat Mitzvah of _____

Honor	Name (English)	Name (Hebrew)
1st Aliyah (Rishon)—a kohen	_____	_____
2nd Aliyah (Sheni)—a levi	_____	_____
3rd Aliyah (Shlishi)	_____	_____
4th Aliyah (Revi'i)	_____	_____
5th Aliyah (Hamishi)	_____	_____
6th Aliyah (Shishi)	_____	_____
7th Aliyah (Shvi'i)	_____	_____
Maftir	_____ (The Bar/Bat Mitzvah Child)	_____
Torah Holder (Hagbah)	_____	_____
Torah Dresser (Glilah)	_____	_____

*Many rules govern who may get an *aliyah* and the order of precedence. Some of these rules are steadfast; others vary from congregation to congregation. Be sure to consult your rabbi for specific information.

Glossary

ALIYAH: literally, "to ascend"; to be called to the Torah. Also refers to moving to Israel.

AMIDAH: Central to every Jewish service is this prayer, said while standing. It contains various blessings of praise, petition, and gratitude.

ASHKENAZIC: literally, "German"; refers to the Eastern European pronunciation of Hebrew. See Sephardic.

ARON HA KODESH: holy ark; the place where the Torah scrolls are kept in the synagogue.

ATARA: the collar on the tallit. By itself it has no inherent religious significance, but it is used to mark one side of the tallit so that the garment is always put on in the same manner.

BET DIN: literally, "House of Judgment"; refers to a Jewish court.

BRIT MILAH: the covenant of circumcision which takes place on the eighth day; also called "bris".

BIMAH: literally, "elevated place." Refers to the platform where the reader's stand for the Torah is placed. Usually the rabbi delivers his sermon from the bimah.

BIRKAT HAMAZON: the blessings at the conclusion of a meal.

CHALLAH: a braided egg bread used for the Sabbath and other occasions; also refers to the portion which is pinched off and symbolically burned for the high priest.

CHANUKIAH: Hebrew for the menorah or candelabrum used for Chanukah, which has eight branches and a Shammash for lighting the other candles.

CHUMASH, pl. CHUMASHIM: literally, "five." Refers to the first five books of the Torah (Genesis, Exodus, Leviticus, Numbers, and Deuteronomy); also the word for the book used during the Shabbat morning service which contains the Torah and Haftarah readings.

D'VAR TORAH or D'RASH: literally, "words of Torah"; a learned speech on some aspect of Torah or Jewish law.

ESTHER, BOOK of: The book read on Purim which tells the story of the Persian King Ahasuerus, his bride Queen Esther, and her uncle Mordechai, who saved the Jews from annihilation by the evil Haman in the fifth century B.C.E.

GABBAI: the honorary synagogue officer who helps organize the service and usually stands on the bimah.

GLILAH: the honor of dressing the Torah Scroll after the Torah reading is completed.

HAFTARAH: the reading from the Prophets following the Torah reading on the Sabbath and festivals.

HAGBAH: the honor of lifting the Torah at the conclusion of the Torah reading.

HALAKHAH: literally, "the way one goes"; the legal and regulatory laws of Judaism.

HALLEL: literally, "praise." Refers to Psalms 113–118 which are included in the services on Rosh Chodesh, Sukkot, Chanukah, Pesach, Shavuot, and Yom Ha'atzmaut.

HASIDIC: literally, "pious." Refers to the devout followers of the Baal Shem Tov, an 18th century mystic. Today there are Hasidic sects, the best known of which is the Lubavitch.

HAVDALAH: literally, "separation"; refers to the ceremony that marks the end of the Sabbath. A special braided candle, sweet spices, and wine are used in this ceremony.

KADDISH: literally, "sanctification." Refers to the prayer used to separate sections of a service, the most famous of which is the mourners' Kaddish. It praises God, proclaims his sovereignty and affirms faith in him.

KASHRUT: Hebrew word for kosher which means "ritually proper" and refers to food prepared in accordance with Jewish law.

KETUVIM: literally, "sacred writings," not from the Torah itself, but considered the third section of the TANACH, an acronym for Torah (Five Books of Moses), Nevi'im (Prophets) and Ketuvim (Writings).

KIDDUSH: literally, "sanctification." Refers to the blessing over the wine on the Sabbath and Festivals. Also, is used to refer to the social gathering at the end of the Sabbath morning service.

KIPAH, pl. KIPOT: Hebrew for yarmulke, the head covering worn by Jews.

KOHEN, pl. KOHANIM: a member of the priestly class; a descendant of Aaron; traditionally one who is given the first aliyah in the Torah reading.

KOHEN GADOL: high priest.

KOTEL: Hebrew for the Western Wall of King Solomon's Temple in Jerusalem; it is the only remaining wall of that structure and is considered one of the holiest places in Jewish history.

LEVITE: members of the Tribe of Levi; in traditional services the person given the second aliyah for the Torah reading.

MAFTIR: the concluding portion of the weekly Torah reading, usually reserved for the Bar/Bat Mitzvah child.

MARRANO: literally, "pig." The name applied to Jews who were forced to convert to Christianity during the Spanish Inquisition in the late 15th century.

MASHGIACH: the person responsible for overseeing that the laws of kashrut are observed during the slaughtering of animals and processing of all food.

MAZEL TOV: good luck.

MEGILLAH: a scroll of papyrus or leather. When used alone it means the Book of Esther.

MIDRASH: commentary on the Torah; sometimes anecdotal or folkloric in nature.

MINCHA: the afternoon prayer service.

MINHAG, pl. MINHAGIM: customs practiced by large segments of the population but which do not have the binding nature of law.

MINYAN: a quorum of ten needed to say certain prayers.

MITZVAH: an obligation or a commandment for adult Jews; commonly used to mean a good deed.

MISHNAH: commentary on the Torah. The Mishnah, together with the Gemara, make up the Talmud.

MOTZI: the blessing over the bread.

NER TAMID: the perpetual lamp that hangs in front of the holy ark.

NEVI'IM: Hebrew for "Prophets." Refers to the prophetic writings from which the weekly Haftarah portion is taken.

OMER: literally, "a sheaf of barley." Refers to the 50 day period between Pesach and Shavuot; traditionally considered a period of mourning when certain restrictions may apply with respect to public celebrations.

ONEG SHABBAT: literally, "the joy of the Sabbath." A social gathering that takes place after the Friday evening service.

PASSOVER, also called PESACH: a holiday beginning on the 15th of Nisan with the seder meal and continuing for 8 days; commemorates the Exodus from Egypt. Since no leaven may be used, many restrictions apply to foods eaten at this time.

PESUKEI D'ZIMRAH: psalms and prayers which introduce the Shabbat morning service.

PIRKE AVOT: literally, "Chapters of the Fathers"; a tractate of Mishnah which consists largely of ethical sayings from individual rabbis.

PURIM: The Festival of Lots which falls on the 14th of Adar. This holiday celebrates the rescue of the Jews from the destruction by Haman who cast lots to determine which day he would kill the Jews. The Jews were eventually saved when Esther, a Jew, convinced her husband Ahasuerus that Haman was evil. The holiday is marked by masquerades, plays, and gifts to the poor (mishloach manot).

ROSH HASHANAH: the Jewish New Year. The holiday is a time for introspection and penitence and hence differs in tone from the celebration of the secular new year.

ROSH HODESH: the first day of a new Jewish month; also a day when the Torah is read.

SEDER: literally, "order"; the ceremonial meal held on the first and/or second night of Passover.

SEFER: the Hebrew word for "book." Also used in reference to the Torah as in "Sefer Torah" meaning the hand-written scroll of the Torah, not a printed book.

SEPHARDIC: Refers to Jews from Spain, North Africa, and Persia. Also refers to the form of pronunciation of Hebrew used in Israel today. See Ashkenazic.

SEUDAH MITZVAH: the festive meal upon completing a Jewish ritual.

SHACHARIT: the morning worship service.

SHAVUOT: the holiday which falls 50 days after Passover and commemorates the giving of the Torah on Mt. Sinai.

SHEMA: the cardinal principle of Judaism, "Hear, O Israel, the Lord our God, the Lord is One."

SHOFAR: a ram's horn sounded several times on Rosh Hashanah and at the conclusion of Yom Kippur, and daily at weekday morning services during the entire month of Elul which preceeds Rosh Hashanah.

SHOMER SHABBAT: literally, "a guardian of the Sabbath"; refers to someone who is religiously observant.

SHULHAN ARUKH: literally, "a prepared table"; the authoritative code of Jewish law written by Joseph Caro in the 16th century.

SIDDUR: the daily, Sabbath, and festival prayer book.

SIDRA: the Torah portion of the week.

SIMCHA: literally, "joy"; meaning a joyous, happy occasion.

SIMCHAT TORAH: the holiday when the annual cycle of Torah reading is completed and the new cycle is immediately begun.

SOFER: a scribe who writes a Torah scroll or other ritual objects.

SUKKAH: literally, a temporary dwelling or hut which has an open roof. Many Jews eat and sleep in their sukkahs for the seven days of the holiday to remind them of Israel's wanderings in the desert.

SUKKOT: called the Festival of Tabernacles or the Festival of Booths which lasts for seven days. It is a pilgrimage festival marking the time of the harvest.

TALLIT: a prayer shawl with fringes (tzitzit) on each of the four corners worn during prayer services. There is also a tallit katan (little prayer shawl) which some Jews wear every day.

TALMUD: the commentary on the Torah. The Talmud is composed of the Mishnah (interpretations on the Torah) and the Gemara (interpretations on the Mishnah).

TANACH: a book containing all sections of the Hebrew Bible; the word is an acronym formed from the first letter of each section, i.e., **T**orah (Five Books of Moses), Nevi'im (Prophets), and **K**etuvim (Writings).

TEFILLAH: the Hebrew word for "prayer."

TEFILLIN: the leather boxes strapped to the head (tefillin shel rosh) and to the arm (tefillin shel yad) which contain quotations from the Bible and are worn during daily morning prayers.

TIKKUN: literally, "to repair"; a book which contains the identical Torah portions printed side-by-side in two different styles, one in the special script from the Torah and the other in modern Hebrew letters with vowels.

TISHA B'AV: the ninth day of the month of Av; observed as a fast day and a day of mourning in memory of the destructions of the two Temples and other calamities in Jewish history.

TORAH: literally, "instruction" or "guidance"; usually meant to refer to the scroll which contains the first five books of the Bible, also called the Five Books of Moses.

TROPE: the melodic notes used in chanting the Torah portion.

TU B'SHEVAT: the 15th of the month of Shevat; the birthday of the trees; usually occurring in late January or early February.

TZEDAKAH: literally, "righteousness" but commonly used to mean charity.

TZITZIT: the blue and white fringes made with a prescribed number of loops and knots attached to the four corners of the tallit or tallit katan.

YAD: literally, "hand." Refers to the hand-shaped pointer used when reading from the Torah since one should not touch the Torah scroll with the bare hand.

YARMULKE: a head covering worn by observant Jews; usually called today by its Hebrew name, "kippah."

YETZER HARA: literally, "evil inclination."

YETZER HATOV: literally, "good inclination."

YOM HA'ATZMAUT: Israel Independence Day which falls on the first of Iyar and marks the reestablishment of the State of Israel in 1948. The day is marked by communal celebrations and special prayers of praise to God.

YOM HA SHOAH: a day of mourning commemorating those who died in the Holocaust.

ZEMIROT: literally, "songs." Refers to the singing at the conclusion of the Sabbath meal.

Selected Books for Further Reference

Cardozo, Arlene. *Jewish Family Celebrations: The Sabbath, Festivals, and Ceremonies.* New York: St. Martin's Press, 1982.

Chiel, Arthur. *Guide to Sidrot and Haftarot.* New York: K'tav, 1971.

Donin, Rabbi Hayim Halevy. *To Be a Jew.* New York: Basic Books, 1972.

———. *To Pray as a Jew.* New York: Basic Books, 1980.

———. *To Raise a Jewish Child.* New York: Basic Books, 1977.

Epstein, David and Stutman, Suzanne. *Torah With Love: A Guide for Strengthening Values Within the Family.* New York: Prentice Hall, 1986.

Freedman, Rabbi E. B. *What Does Being Jewish Mean?* New York: Prentice Hall, 1991.

Greenberg, Blu. *How to Run a Traditional Jewish Household.* New York: Simon and Schuster, 1983.

Greenberg, Irving. *The Jewish Way: Living the Holidays.* New York: Summit, 1988.

Hammer, Rabbi Reuven. *The Other Child in Jewish Education.* New York: United Synagogue, 1979.

Hoffman, Lawrence. *The Art of Public Prayer: Not for Clergy Only.* Washington, DC: Pastoral Press, 1989.

Kling, Simcha. *Embracing Judaism.* New York: Rabbinical Assembly, n.d.

Prager, Dennis and Telushkin, Joseph. *Nine Questions People Ask About Judaism.* New York: Simon and Schuster, 1981.

Rockland, Mae. *The Jewish Party Book: A Contemporary Guide to Customs, Crafts, and Foods.* New York: Schocken Books, 1978.

Salkin, Jeffrey. *Putting God on the Guest List: How to Reclaim the Spiritual Meaning of Your Child's Bar or Bat Mitzvah.* Woodstock, VT: Jewish Lights, 1992.

Sandberg, Martin. *Tefillin: and you shall bind them . . .* United Synagogue Commission on Jewish Education, 1992.

Strassfeld, Michael. *The Jewish Holidays.* New York: Harper and Row, 1985.

Strassfeld, Sharon and Strassfeld, Michael. *The Jewish Catalog.* 3 volumes. Philadelphia: Jewish Publication Society, 1976.

Syme, Daniel. *The Jewish Home*. New York: Union of American Hebrew Congregations, 1988.

Telushkin, Joseph. *Jewish Literacy: The Most Important Things to Know about the Jewish Religion, Its People and Its History*. New York: William Morrow, 1991.

Trepp, Leo. *The Complete Book of Jewish Observance: A Practical Manual for the Modern Jew*. New York: Behrman House, 1980.

Index

About the Authors:

Jane Lewit is a graduate of Wellesley College and Harvard University. She has a Masters in Jewish Education from American University. As a professional Jewish educator, she works with synagogue schools, Hebrew literacy programs, and adult education. **Ellen Epstein** graduated from Connecticut College for Women and attended the University of London. She is an oral historian and the co-author of *Record and Remember: Tracing Your Roots Through Oral History*. For the past 20 years she has run her own business, The Center For Oral History. The two authors have collectively planned eight bar and bat mitzvah celebrations for their own children and have consulted with friends and family on countless other occasions.